GHOSTS OF CONCORD'S COLONIAL INN

SAM BALTRUSIS

FOREWORD BY JONI MAYHAN

Haunted America

Published by Haunted America
A Division of The History Press
Charleston, SC
www.historypress.com

First published 2023

Manufactured in the United States

ISBN 9781467153980

Library of Congress Control Number: 2023934800

CONTENTS

CONTENTS

FOREWORD

Sometimes a haunting isn't what you expect.

There are various ways to investigate reports of paranormal activity. Some teams will research the destination thoroughly and go in armed with information. Other investigators, myself included, always try to go into locations with open minds and clean slates. If we don't know what to expect, we aren't trying to make the evidence we collect fit a specific narrative. We will ask our questions and collect our data from scratch. If it lines up with what others have found, we'll take that as a win, but it doesn't always happen that way.

Many times, we can't avoid knowing the history of the building. If it's a popular paranormal hotspot, we'll know about it and will arrive with preconceived notions. Concord's Colonial Inn is a good example.

There is simply no way of walking into the building without the understanding that it played a role in the American Revolution. It is within shouting distance of the Old North Bridge, where the "shot heard 'round the world" occurred, and is surrounded by numerous landmarks and historical markers. In addition, the inn has been on several paranormal television shows, including the original *Ghost Hunters*.

Ten years ago, my paranormal team rented three rooms at Concord's Colonial Inn and obtained permission to conduct an investigation. Many of us in the group were budding mediums and were excited about the prospects. We fully expected to encounter Revolutionary War soldiers or even patrons from that period. While we did encounter a soldier in room 24, I also had an experience that left me perplexed. I ran into a contemporary ghost.

The original structure of Concord's Colonial Inn, which currently serves as the front desk and Liberty restaurant, was built in 1716. *Courtesy of the Boston Public Library, Print Department.*

I found her quite by accident. At one point during the investigation, I left the room we'd rented and began exploring an upstairs hallway. As I rounded the corner, I felt a strong presence lingering directly in front of me. It was a young woman. She was dark-haired and frantic. Her energy was hysterical and difficult to interpret. Something bad had happened to her, and she was still caught in that moment. While I didn't actually see her, I felt her and saw a clear picture of her in my mind. I quickly pulled out my digital recorder and turned it on, capturing a faint plea. "Help," was all she told me.

I tried to communicate with her, but she darted away, and I couldn't find her again. She stayed on my mind though. Who was she, and why was she haunting Concord's Colonial Inn?

I didn't think she was a guest, and she was far too contemporary to be part of the inn's early history. The mind picture I saw showed me a woman from the 1960s. How did she get there? Why did she remain?

In some ways, it was a true paradox. I felt strongly that she didn't have any ties to the inn, but yet, there she was, haunting the building. This is something that has come up on numerous investigations. Why do ghosts haunt specific buildings?

In the decade since I first investigated the inn, I've learned a thing or two. The biggest misconception? People do not need to die at the location in order to haunt it. Sometimes they drift in with no explanation.

I've seen this at dozens of haunted locations. We will find the ghosts we expect to find but then also discover others who have no ties to the property. In some ways, the location becomes a "ghost hotel," becoming more and more haunted as time passes.

Sam Baltrusis and I have been friends for years, and we've discussed this many times, trying to make sense of it. One factor we've landed on that makes perfect sense is that investigators often bring ghosts to locations. Ghosts are frequently drawn to people who are aware of them and will sometimes follow them to the next investigation. Once they're there, the ghosts might find something even more compelling at the location and make the decision to stay.

Something else I've learned over the years is to be patient. Sometimes the information will present itself to me at a later date. And this is exactly what happened. A decade later, as Sam began investigating the haunting at Concord's Colonial Inn, he also encountered the mystery woman. Not only did he see her in the same location where I found her, but he also saw her as

The Old North Bridge in Concord is often referred to as the location of the "shot heard 'round the world" and the beginning of the American Revolution. *Courtesy of the Boston Public Library, Print Department.*

Room 24 located on the second floor of Concord's Colonial Inn is often considered to be the hotel's most haunted. *Courtesy of Concord's Colonial Inn.*

a frantic young woman with dark hair. When we compared notes, a chill ran up my spine. There was no doubt we both stumbled across the same woman.

Why was she there? What had happened to her?

Luckily for me, the answers would eventually present themselves. Sam is an excellent researcher and soon began the journey of attempting to identify her. The haunting at Concord's Colonial Inn is deep and mysterious, commanding layers of intrigue. If anyone can get to the bottom of it, Sam will be the one.

Joni Mayhan is a paranormal investigator and the author of twenty-four paranormal books. She owns and operates Haunted New Harmony Ghost Walks and Investigations in New Harmony, Indiana, where she currently lives. Visit JoniMayhan.com for more information.

ACKNOWLEDGEMENTS

If a ghost is history demanding to be remembered, then the spirits rumored to hang out at Old North Bridge where the American Revolution first erupted on April 19, 1775, were in hibernation.

Yes, they were taking a "boo" break.

During a series of visits where the "shot heard 'round the world" was fired, I was initially surprised that many of the historical locations in Concord and Lexington—like Buckman Tavern and the Battle Green—had very few reports of ghostly activity. One tour guide in Lexington supposedly spotted an apparition of a colonial-era woman on the Buckman Tavern's second floor, and another person swore they heard phantom footsteps at the Sanderson House.

At the time, I remember thinking that all of the Revolutionary War–era spirits must have headed over to Concord's Colonial Inn.

And yes, I was right.

It was during this period I met Zachary Trznadel, the former front desk manager at Concord's Colonial Inn, who introduced me to the legend and lore associated with the inn. When I would book a getaway to Concord, he would always upgrade me into one of the allegedly haunted rooms. We would then talk about my experiences, and he would later become a major resource quoted throughout *Ghosts of Concord's Colonial Inn*.

In January 2022, Trznadel hired me as a night auditor so I could immerse myself in the history and mystery of the inn. My six-month stint working the graveyard shift didn't disappoint. In fact, I had several firsthand experiences

The North Bridge, often referred to as the Old North Bridge, is a historic site in Concord. *Courtesy of the Boston Public Library, Print Department.*

with the ghosts of Concord's Colonial Inn and spoke to dozens of guests who also believed the inn was a hotbed of paranormal activity.

As noted in the text, Trznadel wrote the section about the inn's history along with local historian Beth van Duzer.

I'm grateful for all the people I interviewed for this book in addition to Trznadel, including Richard Estep, Brian Cano, Chris Fleming, Gare Allen, Peter Muise, Michelle Hamilton, Geoffrey Campbell, Tim Weisberg, James Annitto, Mike Ricksecker, Michael Baker, Gavin Kleespies and Jeremy Cotter. I would also like to thank the staff at the historic hotel for their continued hospitality and support while writing *Ghosts of Concord's Colonial Inn.*

Many of the photos featured in this book were supplied by the general manager, Alek Adamson, and appear courtesy of Concord's Colonial Inn. Photographers Frank C. Grace and Jason Baker also deserve shout-outs for their work.

Special thanks to Joni Mayhan for penning the book's foreword. Thomas D'Agostino and Arlene Nicholson from Dining with the Dead 1031 deserve major props for inviting me to guest co-host their series of spirited events at the inn. Mayhan, D'Agostino and Nicholson are also featured throughout the book.

I would like to thank Mike Kinsella from The History Press/Arcadia for his support during the process of putting *Ghosts of Concord's Colonial Inn* together.

In addition to connecting with the inn's ghosts, I was able to spend quality time with so many amazing guests—ranging from the cast and crew from *The Parenting* movie to history buffs from all over the country to long-term residents like my friend Carol, who kept me company at the front desk when the lights would mysteriously go out.

For those who love Concord's Colonial Inn as much as I do, this book is for you.

INTRODUCTION

My first spirited overnight stay at Concord's Colonial Inn was in October 2018. I was on the hunt for haunted locations for an upcoming paranormal convention spotlighting the famous authors who lived and died in this peaceful transcendentalist enclave in Massachusetts. When I checked into Concord's Colonial Inn, I was immediately overwhelmed with the lingering energy of the ghosts of the city's tumultuous past.

It was love at first sight.

The spirits of Concord called me. And it was more than the psychic imprint left by the "shot heard 'round the world." The residual energy haunting the inn spans more than three centuries. Based on my initial baseline sweep of the property, several of the ghosts sticking around simply didn't know that they were dead.

"Imagine waking up in the middle of the night to find a Revolutionary War soldier standing at the foot of your bed," author Joni Mayhan warned me before my visit to Concord's Colonial Inn. "Built in 1716, the inn is located just down the road from the North Bridge, where the Battles of Lexington and Concord occurred. During the Revolutionary War, a portion of the inn was used to store firearms and provisions for the militia. Another section was the office of Dr. Timothy Minot. Wounded soldiers were brought to his office during the battle, and many succumbed to their injuries, lending truth to the ghostly encounters."

Converted to an inn around 1889 and renamed Concord's Colonial Inn eleven years later, the hotel was home to Henry David Thoreau, famous

Concord's Colonial Inn became a hotel in 1889 and was originally called the Colonial House. The building was formerly three separate constructions and was combined into one in 1897. *Courtesy of Concord's Colonial Inn.*

for his "Civil Disobedience" essay and, of course, *Walden*. Thoreau lived with his aunts while he attended Harvard. The eighteenth-century structure served as a boardinghouse before being transformed into a hotel called the Thoreau House, named after the famous writer's aunts.

"When I had the opportunity to investigate the inn years ago, I wasn't disappointed by the activity," Mayhan told me. "While we didn't see the soldier materialize in the bedroom, we did witness strange tapping sounds, shadows moving and odd smells appearing out of nowhere. While conducting an electronic voice phenomenon, or EVP, session in an attempt to get the resident ghosts to speak to us through our digital recorders, a lacy doily flew off the back of a chair and landed on my head, surprising me."

After checking into my supposedly non-haunted room located in the Prescott wing of the hotel, I had a long conversation with the Colonial Inn's former night auditor, Aaron. His own personal experience with the notoriously haunted inn's ghosts involved a radio turning on by itself. No surprise, but there were no batteries in the electronic device.

As the conversation progressed, the front desk employee told me that a guest checked into the haunted room 24 during his shift. According to his story, the woman fled her room with a "boo!" within ten minutes after she

Author Sam Baltrusis worked the overnight shift at Concord's Colonial Inn for six months to immerse himself in the historically haunted hotel's history and ghost lore. *Photo by Frank C. Grace.*

said the lights in the room mysteriously turned off and a disembodied voice said, "Get out." Of course, the freaked-out guest did.

The night auditor mentioned that employees often hear voices in the inn's main dining area called Merchants Row. "The older employees always seem to experience the inn's ghosts," he told me. "Not the younger workers."

Aaron told me that he feels uncomfortable walking into the main restaurant, Merchants Row, at night. "I can't explain it, but it feels like I'm walking into a den of bears." Apparently, Aaron doesn't want to poke the bear. I asked if employees had spotted an elderly female spirit in the hotel, and he confirmed my hunch. Aaron said she has been spotted lounging in a chair in the sitting room on the main floor next to the creepy paintings. When I walked by, I got the chills because I could see her in my mind's eye.

After my chat with Aaron, I decided to check out Concord at night and walked to the nearby Old Hill Burying Ground in Monument Square. Originally next to Concord's first meetinghouse, the graveyard is more than three hundred years old. According to superstition, it was bad luck to transport a corpse over flowing water, so the community created South Burying Ground on the opposite side of Mill Brook. For years, the Monument Square cemetery was known as North Burying Ground.

As soon as I walked up to the historic cemetery, I felt like I was being watched. In fact, I somehow picked up something sinister from what locals call the "skull tombstone" at Old Hill Burying Ground. "According to the lore, there's an eerie aura throughout the 1700s burying ground," reported *Concord Patch*'s Patrick Ball. "The spookiest site is an old tombstone with a strange skull image and equally unsettling 'bowing to the king of terror' inscription. Some report seeing 'real' eyes inside the skull's sockets, which appear to follow visitors as they move around."

After my midnight stroll, I headed back to Concord's Colonial Inn to report on my "creepy as hell" experiences out in the cemetery. As soon as I walked into my room and turned on my computer, I intuitively knew that I wasn't alone. Holding my trusty dowsing rods charged for spirit communication, I set up an online video chat with my friends on social media. I was hoping that my fellow empaths from the psychic community could figure out who, or what, was in the hotel room with me.

Oddly, my computer kept turning on and off. Issues with electronic devices, based on firsthand experience, are usually a sign that something wicked this way comes.

"There's a woman in the room," chimed in one of my spirit medium friends with the ability to remotely see the ghosts that I connect with at some

The middle section of Concord's Colonial Inn, today's main inn, was used as an ammunition store during the American Revolution and played a pivotal role in the Battles of Lexington and Concord. *Courtesy of the Boston Public Library, Print Department.*

of New England's most haunted locations. "She's in the corner not wanting to be seen or heard. She's just curious."

The psychics watching the live feed believed the spirit was possibly a nurse from the eighteenth century. However, my computer screen kept freezing, and my friends were picking up all sorts of conflicting activity. "What happened to the video feed? I was going to say that the spirit is related to something medical," commented a fellow empath. "She was a midwife in her forties."

Several people watching the live video told me that the entity kept changing form and was possibly a shapeshifter. The spirit medium warned, "Do you know that you're talking to a trickster?"

The spirit medium was right. When I asked the entity to present itself to me, I realized that I was connecting with a crone, an elderly woman often portrayed in pop culture as a wise witch with magical powers. Apparently, the entity had a sense of humor. "Could you be more stereotypical?" I joked with the shapeshifting entity. She cackled.

Several of my psychic friends who watched the series of online videos recommended that I leave the inn immediately. "She's intrigued by your energy," said psychic Kristen Cappucci. "She will try to mess with you tonight."

After communicating with the witch ghost, I headed downstairs for some fresh air because I couldn't sleep. As I walked into the lobby area, I clearly heard a male voice whisper in my ear. "Right behind you," he said. I jumped. "Oh, you scared me," I said, totally relieved…well, for a split second.

I turned around, and there was nobody there. The night auditor was on the second floor. I was completely creeped out, but I was exhausted. I decided to crash in my room for the night despite multiple warnings from my psychic-medium friends.

As I tossed and turned in my bed, the crone wouldn't leave me alone. She kept sitting on my chest. Known as a "night hag," the malevolent entity from folklore has been associated with sleep paralysis or night terrors. It's a phenomenon of feeling immobilized by an unseen force.

The traumatic night was on replay and repeated itself several times throughout my sleep. I would wake up, unable to move and feeling as if I was pinned to the bed. Finally, after an intense struggle and raising myself from the bed, I would gasp for air. After about three visits from the night hag, I begged her to leave me alone. She eventually listened.

I managed to get about an hour of sleep. Witch, please.

Author Joni Mayhan didn't encounter the ghost witch when she investigated the overnight haunt years ago; however, she did communicate with a Revolutionary War–era soldier. "Guests of the inn have witnessed this soldier walking into their room in the middle of the night. They see him as a wispy apparition in shades of black and white. After he comes into the room, he stands at the foot of the bed before dissipating into thin air. This was the first room we investigated," she recalled.

Mayhan said that she investigated the inn early in her paranormal career. "There were five of us scattered around the room. We dimmed the lights, turned on our digital recorders and sat silently for a moment. The room buzzed with paranormal energy. You could feel it hanging in the air like a current of electricity. When he drifted in, I felt him immediately."

During the investigation, Mayhan said that she heard what sounded like a faint response from the spirit on her digital recorder. "Every one of us picked up on the fact that he was a soldier. This wasn't surprising because we came into the room with this one piece of information. What interested me were the descriptions. We didn't know what he looked like prior to the investigation. We only knew that he presented himself in shades of black and white. Every single medium described him as having dark blond hair that was longish and unkempt. Three out of the five of us saw him with a head wound, one that probably took his life, and we all were certain that he wasn't aware he was dead," she said. "With this knowledge, we attempted to cross him over, but he refused to go. He was still trapped in the battle, intent on finishing his mission. He dismissed us and promptly disappeared into the night."

When asked why Concord's Colonial Inn is so haunted, Mayhan told me that there's an "aura of disaster" psychically embedded in the land.

The painting located in the lobby of Concord's Colonial Inn pays homage to the Minute Man statue by Daniel Chester French and commemorates the fallen militiamen who fought on April 19, 1775. *Photo by Sam Baltrusis.*

"I believe the haunting of the Concord Colonial Inn is primarily due to the residual energy effect. There were countless traumas that happened in the area, resulting in horrific deaths," she said. "Emotions also played a tremendous role. People fought hard for what they believed in, and they gave their lives for the cause. The land recorded this event, providing residual energy, while the earthbound souls remained there, reliving their deaths over and over again."

There was something about my first night at Concord's Colonial Inn that inspired dozens of repeat visits and ultimately a stint as the inn's night auditor starting in January 2022. I wanted more. There was something inexplicable pushing me to dig deeper into the skeletal secrets lurking in the shadows of this historic hotel.

Back in 2018, I had no idea I had stumbled upon a labyrinthine crypt of unsolved mysteries and paranormal activity. The ghosts of Concord's Colonial Inn needed postmortem peace, and they had summoned me to somehow help them find closure.

What intrigues me the most, however, is the more that I looked into the Colonial Inn and its history, the more questions I had about the place. This book is my attempt to answer some of them.

TIMELINE

A rmed with the idea that a ghost is history demanding to be remembered, I felt an intense calling to redirect my paranormal lens toward Concord, Massachusetts.

After my initial stay in 2018, I spent a series of overnights in the haunted rooms at the Colonial Inn. The trek on the commuter rail started to become a regular getaway when I needed to take a break from the hustle and bustle of city living. During this period, I even filmed a segment for the Travel Channel's *Fright Club* recorded remotely on my computer from my room in the main inn. On the paranormal-themed program with Jack Osbourne and the Ghost Brothers, I was asked to give my expert take on a video clip involving a shadow figure caught on camera at a crime museum in Florida.

My experiences with the inn's ghosts were limited at first, but I knew they were there. It felt like they were playing hide-and-seek with me. As I continued to immerse myself in the legends and lore of the inn, the mysterious messages from the other side of the veil slowly started to manifest. One spirited night in March 2020 involved phantom footsteps under a full moon on Old North Bridge.

While taking a midnight stroll to the location where the first shots were fired that ultimately ignited the powder keg known as the American Revolution, I heard what sounded like heavy footsteps marching over the bridge as if they were walking over to me. No one was there. What was even more strange with the situation was that the ghostly clopping sounds stormed right by me as if they didn't even know I was there.

Concord's Colonial Inn has a connection with Henry David Thoreau, whose grandfather built its eastern section. It was inherited by Thoreau's father in 1801, and the author of *Walden* later stayed at the inn for two years while studying at Harvard University. *Photo by Detroit Publishing Company.*

Residual redcoats? Yes, Concord has them.

This began a series of visitations from what I believe was the ghost of a wounded British soldier. One night while staying in room 24 at the inn, I saw what looked like a black shadow of a man crawl on the ground from the bathroom and dissipate in front of the room's fireplace. It seemed to be residual in nature, almost like an endless "ghost loop" or a video replay of something that had happened in the past.

When I saw the crawling shadow figure, I started asking questions using my dowsing rods to hopefully get some answers.

"Are you a wounded soldier?" I asked out loud using my copper "witch sticks." They crossed both times, implying a definite "yes." "Were you a colonist?" The rods didn't cross, indicating "no." I then asked if the spirit was British. The dowsing rods not only crossed but also started to spin almost like a helicopter propeller. I was on to something.

There's a makeshift memorial across the street from Concord's Colonial Inn honoring the fallen British soldier who died while being transported from Old North Bridge to the temporary hospital manned by Dr. Timothy Minot. *Photo by Sam Baltrusis.*

For New Year's Eve 2020, I decided to do another overnight at the inn. I normally stayed in what was considered the haunted wing of the structure near room 24. For my last haunted hurrah in 2020, I stayed in the east side of the structure formerly owned by Henry David Thoreau's family, including his aunts Sarah and Elizabeth. In fact, it's believed that Thoreau lived in what is now room 3.

When I asked Concord Colonial Inn's front desk manager, Zachary Trznadel, if there were any reports about the east side of the property, he said that there are many sightings of what many believe was one of Thoreau's aunts.

I then asked him if there was any backstory about a wounded soldier with unfinished business on the east side of the inn. He sheepishly nodded. "Ammi White owned that side of the property," Trznadel told me. "There's a whole bloody backstory involving him and a British soldier."

My chin dropped.

I then had an epiphany related to the wounded soldier whom I encountered first at the Old North Bridge and then in my room at Concord's Colonial Inn. I strongly believed that it was related to a hatchet murder that included a reported scalping and dismemberment committed by Ammi White, who actually owned the eastern portion of the property years after the Revolutionary War. The British used the murder as propaganda to portray the Patriot militia as savages. Was it a mercy killing or act of barbaric murder?

Intrigued by the mystery involving Ammi White, I had a long chat with Zachary about the inn's history. "The Colonial was originally three separate buildings," he told me. "The oldest section of the inn dates back to 1716," he said, pointing to the gift shop and the front portion of what is now the Liberty Room dining area. This spirited discussion led to many more repeat visits to this Sleepy Hollow–esque enclave and eventually a part-time position as a night auditor at the historic inn.

Each of the three buildings that compose Concord's Colonial Inn was known by a different name throughout its storied history. For clarity, I'm referring to them as the East House, the Central Building and the West House.

Pulled from information compiled by the staff at Concord's Colonial Inn, here's a timeline of the property's history spanning more than three hundred years:

Prior to 1663: The land was owned by Peter Bulkeley, one of Concord's original settlers.

1663: The land was sold by Peter Bulkeley's widow, Grace, to Captain Timothy Wheeler.

1687: Captain Wheeler left his land to his daughter Rebecca, wife of Captain James Minot (1653–1735).

Late 1600s: James Minot built the East House. The exact date isn't known, but there are records that he lived in the house prior to November 14, 1716.

1716: Captain Minot deeded this East House to his son James.

1759: James Jr. died and left the "dwelling house, barns and all of the other buildings on the home lot to my son Ephraim."

1764, January 20: Ephraim sold the property to his cousin Timothy Minot Jr. (1726–1804) coupled with twenty acres bounded on the west by the Millbrook. According to local legend, Dr. Minot tended to the wounded at his homestead in Monument Square along with Dr. John Cuming, who set up a makeshift hospital for the British wounded at the Daniel Bliss house on April 19, 1775.

1766: Dr. Minot mortgaged the property to another cousin, Samuel Minot, a goldsmith from Boston. The mortgage was discharged in 1770.

1770–75: During the Minot ownership, the Central Building was erected at the west end of East House. It was described by townspeople as a one-story, heavily timbered structure. It was used as a provincial storehouse during the American Revolution.

1780: Deacon John White rented the new building for a store and lived in one end of it. He soon added a second story and moved upstairs. The store specialized in paints and oils but also carried general merchandise; the sign said "Variety Store."

1789: Dr. Timothy Minot Jr. sold the East House to Ammi White, the cabinetmaker, who, as a boy, was the one who killed the third British soldier at the bridge with an axe. He was the son-in-law of Dr. Minot and added a long shop, or shed, to his East House. On this same day, Dr. Minot sold the Central Building to Deacon White.

1799, October 30: Ammi White sold his East House to John Thoreau (1754–1801) a Boston-based merchant, and a parcel of land as well as the additional shed. The deacon's wife next door was the sister of John Thoreau's second wife, Rebecca Kettel. The brothers of Esther and Rebecca ran the bakery in Wright Tavern in neighboring Lexington, Massachusetts.

1801: Thoreau died, and his widow and children, including fourteen-year-old John, continued residence in the East House with John Sr.'s two sisters: Sarah, a town seamstress, and Elizabeth (Betsy), who inherited the house. The boy John (1788–1859) worked as a clerk in the store for a while. He became Henry David Thoreau's father.

1812: The Central Building, or store, passed from Deacon White to Bela Hemenway and Daniel Shattuck, but White retained an interest in the store.

1820: About this date, Deacon White built a duplicate section at the west end of the store for his own house. According to reports, he would stop people from traveling on Sunday and was especially strict about Lowell Road.

1821: Daniel Shattuck, partner of Deacon White, who had been living above the store, bought the shop and stock from White.

1830: Deacon White (Unitarian Church, 1784–1827) died. Shattuck bought the West House and moved into it. Dan Shattuck helped found the Middlesex Insurance Company, National Bank and Savings Bank. His brother Lemuel, who had been helping with the store since 1823, moved into the rooms above the store, where he remained until 1833, when he moved to Boston to become a book publisher. Lemuel wrote the first history of Concord. He presented the first report ever given at a town meeting and got a law passed making such reports mandatory throughout the state. He was the founder of the American Statistical Society and the New England Genealogy Society.

1835–37: Henry David Thoreau, his parents, sisters and brothers lived on the property with aunts Betsy and Sarah. Henry lived in the house while he was a student at Harvard in Cambridge, Massachusetts.

1839: Betsy Thoreau died. Dan Shattuck bought the East House. Eventually, it was occupied by R.N. Rice, Mrs. Barlow, the Tolmans, F.S. Simonds and many other tenants until 1885. Rueben Rice was manager of the Green Store, where the Catholic church now stands, and then he went west to work for the railroads; he returned to Concord as a town financial benefactor. F.S. Simonds was the author of several history books.

1850: Shattuck made over the whole store building into a dwelling, which he rented to John F. Skinner. It was known as the Skinner House until late 1893. Dan Shattuck used the timbers of Deacon White's barn to build an ell on the Lowell Road side and a stable for himself. These were famous timbers cut for the meetinghouse built in 1667 and removed in 1710 when a new meetinghouse was built to erect a structure for courts and town meetings on the south side of the common. Deacon White moved this old court building to the rear of his West House for a barn.

1855: The Central Building became a boardinghouse. Soon this building was attached to East House, and the combination was run as a small hotel called Thoreau House. It was operated by several people, including Thatcher Magoun, W.E. Rand and J. Tarleton.

1861: Dan Shattuck was still living in West House, but with his daughter Frances, who was married to Louis A. Surette Jr. He deeded her the property, which included East House. Surette's son Thomas became a famous musician.

1865: East House was owned by the town's trustees and served as housing for boarders.

1900: During this period, the West House was attached to the Central Building. It was managed by the Abrams family, who rebranded the entire property as the Colonial Inn.

1947: Ownership of Concord's Colonial Inn was taken over by the Grimes brothers, Luther and Loring. For seventeen years, Loring was resident

Residence of Store Keeper.   Old Provincial Store during   Residence of Henry D. Thoreau's
                              Revolutionary Times.   Grandfather, built by him, 1770.
NOW THE COLONIAL INN, CONCORD, MASS.

Three of Concord's historic houses, referred to as the East House, the Central Building and the West House in the timeline, were joined to form the Colonial Inn's current structure. *Courtesy of the Boston Public Library, Print Department.*

director, and he added the Prescott wing in 1960 and the Merchants Row dining room in 1973.

1988: When hotelier Jurgen Demisch became proprietor in 1988, he soon recognized the importance of the inn as a historical landmark. Major renovations and redecoration of the inn took place with his wife, Rebecca, and it became a hotspot known for its restaurants and customer service.

2015: Demisch sold the inn to former congressman Michael Harrington, proprietor of the Hawthorne Hotel in Salem and the Publick House in Sturbridge, Massachusetts. Today, Concord's Colonial Inn is listed in the National Register of Historic Places and is a proud member of the National Trust for Historic Preservation's Historic Hotels of America.

THE HISTORY

Concord transforms from a sleepy New England village to a nerve center of activity in the days leading up to the anniversary of the "shot heard 'round the world." Patriots Day weekend is a big deal in Massachusetts and manages to attract American Revolutionary War history buffs from all over the country, as well as the thousands of spectators and runners who travel to the Bay State to participate in the Boston Marathon.

From a paranormal perspective, one can definitely feel the energy shift at Concord's Colonial Inn during this annual commemoration. Many of the guests staying at the inn are in town to either participate in the various reenactments around North Bridge or watch from the sidelines. During the festivities, it is the norm to spot revelers wearing tricorn hats and period-specific garb while downing ales with their mates at the inn's Forge Tavern.

During the weeklong celebration, it feels like the veil between the living and the dead has been lifted. Gary Mosby, a guest from California who visited during Patriots Day weekend in 2022, agreed based on an experience he had at Concord's Colonial Inn more than two decades ago. During a chat we had at the front desk while he was checking in, Mosby wasn't able to shake the image from his mind.

"It's been twenty years and I've only seen one ghost in my lifetime, and it was here," he said, excited to be back at the Colonial after all these years. "I strongly believe he was one of the Revolutionary War soldiers that may have been keeping guard of the ammunition stored here." When asked if the soldier he encountered was possibly someone of note, like Paul Revere,

Left: The area that became the town of Concord was originally known as Musketaquid, an Algonquian word for "grassy plain." Concord was established in 1635 by a group of English settlers. *Courtesy of Concord's Colonial Inn.*

Opposite: Wright's Tavern was built in 1747 by Ephraim Jones, who operated it until 1751. At the dawn of the American Revolution in April 1775, it was managed by Amos Wright and served as a nerve center of activity during the Battles of Lexington and Concord. *Photo by Detroit Publishing Company.*

he shook his head "no." "He had dark hair that was in a ponytail and brown knickers and blue jacket."

While I was chatting with Mosby and his wife, I shared with them an experience I had while working the overnight shift at Concord's Colonial Inn. A few nights before the big Patriots Day Parade on Monday, April 18, 2022, in Monument Square, I clearly heard what sounded like phantom cannon explosions in the wee hours of the night. When I checked with my friend Geoffrey Campbell, a Plymouth-based reenactor, he confirmed that no cannons were shot in Concord or Lexington.

"Based on my experience, I will say that a cannon fire at that hour is highly unlikely unless you're talking about the reenactment at Lexington Green that starts around 4:30 a.m.," he told me. "That's the only event that has firing of any sort in the early morning hours. Revere's ride takes place overnight, but there's no musket or cannon fire."

When it comes to paranormal activity associated with the American Revolution, Campbell is my go-to guy. In addition to leading ghost tours throughout "America's Hometown" as the owner and operator of Plymouth Night Tour, Campbell is the commander of the End Zone Militia, a group of rebel reenactors responsible for holding down the fort at New England Patriots games.

Campbell and his crew of musket-wielding minutemen get to play dress-up at Gillette Stadium. "Some of the weirdest moments I've had are

when you suddenly realize that you're experiencing something exactly as another person would have 250 years ago," Campbell told me. "It's like time travel."

During the off-season, Campbell dons his tricorn cap for special gatherings at historic Revolutionary War–era sites scattered throughout New England. "Whether it's on a battlefield, in an encampment, laying on a blanket looking up at the stars with no man-made lights, it's beautiful and amazing," he told me. "If you add the paranormal and ghostly aspect on top of it, then it can be downright freaky."

Campbell said that he has heard about paranormal activity near North Bridge and had one sleepless night at Concord's Colonial Inn. "I've always been curious about some of the sites along Battle Road, especially Bloody Angle, inside the park. Definitely would like to do an investigation there sometime to see if any of the eight British soldiers killed there continue to linger," he said. "However, my only experience was at Concord's Colonial Inn. I had my covers pulled up one night when I was staying over."

When asked if Revolutionary War reenactors could somehow trigger residual hauntings during the Patriots Day celebration, Campbell nodded in agreement. "Of course," he explained. "We dress and try to act like people of that time did. It makes total sense that a spirit of that time would be attracted to us or question who we really are. They also could mistake us for someone they knew."

Campbell believes that many of the spirits sticking around Concord don't actually know that they have passed. "Sometimes I question whether these spirits realize they're dead and that the war is long over," he said. "Based on personal experience, it's quite eerie to sit on a hill at night and hear rattling metal and disembodied voices calling for water and their mothers."

A few days after the Patriots Day parade, I followed up with Gary Mosby and his wife as they were checking out of Concord's Colonial Inn. I asked him if he had seen the Patriot ghost during his stay, and he shook his head "no." He did, however, have a spirited time exploring the various sites and sounds, including the Minuteman National Historic Park.

When Gary gave me a detailed description of the 1700s-era ghost man he spotted years ago, it reminded me of an experience I had in December 2020 while staying as a guest in room 24. I clearly remember seeing a shadow figure emerge from a dark alley next to the Masonic Lodge across the street.

That fateful night, I was outside in front of Monument Square. I heard what sounded like horse hooves galloping on the street, and I looked to my right and clearly saw a shadow figure with what appeared to be a soldier's hat. Based on what I could surmise from the spirit, he appeared to be wounded. There was a sadness emanating from the specter, and I wanted to help him. If I had to describe the entity, he seemed to be what I would call a "watcher." He was just standing there. Waiting.

Forge Tavern, located in the middle section of the historic inn, is believed to be the spot where the militia stored arms and provisions for the Concord minutemen. *Courtesy of Concord's Colonial Inn.*

After retelling the story to my new friend from California, I remembered one key aspect of my ghostly encounter in 2020. The shadow soldier seemed to be pointing at something.

My overnight auditor shift at Concord's Colonial Inn ended at 7:00 a.m., and I quickly walked over to the spot where I first saw the entity. As I inspected the walkway next to the Masonic Lodge, I got an intense spirit message to "look" and then turned around and headed down Monument Street. It was at this point that I spotted what appeared to be a stone marker with a Union flag next to it right across the street.

How did I miss this before? It's a makeshift memorial for a fallen British soldier who was killed on April 19, 1775, at North Bridge. I gasped. It's him. I knew it.

When I acknowledged him and then performed a crossing prayer, I felt a cold spot rise around me. I'm so grateful that I was able to communicate with this man and hopefully find him some postmortem peace. As soon as I said goodbye to the fallen soldier, it started to rain. I was shivering in the beauty and the madness of the moment. It was an incredibly moving experience.

BATTLES OF LEXINGTON AND CONCORD

When it comes to the "shot heard 'round the world" on April 19, 1775, there's been a two-hundred-year-old war of words between the towns of Lexington and Concord that's never seen a ceasefire. The centuries-old battle over which town should get credit for being the initial spark that ignited the American Revolution has been an ongoing debate since at least 1820.

Yes, it's a battle over the battle. Of course, the town rivalry intensified when Ralph Waldo Emerson's famous "Concord Hymn" sided with his hometown in 1837.

The tensions date back to the era when Revolutionary War hero Marquis de Lafayette toured the country and raised the consciousness of the importance of that initial skirmish. The two towns then engaged in a "pamphlet war" in the early 1800s glorifying their roles in the initial battle and throwing dirt at their neighbors.

The Lexington versus Concord debate was so intense that it stymied a visit from President Ulysses S. Grant in April 1875. He tried his best to be diplomatic by having lunch in both towns, but the war of words continued.

Was the "shot heard 'round the world" in Lexington or Concord? It's not an open-and-shut case.

The minuteman statue near Old North Bridge is set near the spot where the first colonial militiamen were killed on April 19, 1775. *Photo by Sam Baltrusis.*

The initial skirmish definitely took place in Lexington Center before Concord, but the militia was told not to fire until the British shot at them. Historians aren't sure if the colonists fired back in Lexington, but they do agree that the first organized shots of the battle happened around Concord's North Bridge.

According to History.com, eight colonists were killed in Lexington Center and nine were wounded, while only one redcoat was injured. "The

British then continued into Concord to search for arms, not realizing that the vast majority had already been relocated," reported History.com. "They decided to burn what little they found, and the fire got slightly out of control. Hundreds of militiamen occupying the high ground outside of Concord incorrectly thought the whole town would be torched. The militiamen hustled to Concord's North Bridge, which was being defended by a contingent of British soldiers. The British fired first but fell back when the colonists returned the volley."

Based on the lack of British casualties in Lexington, the first shots in retaliation coming from the colonists likely occurred in Concord.

Mystery solved? Not so fast.

If we are searching for the historical truth, the first shots fired in protest actually happened in Somerville, Massachusetts, on September 1, 1774, in a precursor to the Revolutionary War known as the "Powder Alarm." In 1774, the British military governor, General Thomas Gage, confiscated the 250 barrels of gunpowder stored in what is now known as Somerville's Old Powder House so that the ammunition wouldn't be used by the Patriots during the Revolutionary War. Musket-toting colonists—ticked off by Gage's orders to steal the powder—made their way to Cambridge, ready to fight. According to *Somerville, Past and Present*, an estimated fifty thousand armed men from across the colonies responded to the word-of-mouth alarm. Shots were definitely fired in protest.

Ten years before the Battles of Lexington and Concord, Gage was appointed as the commander-in-chief of the British forces in North America, which was the highest-ranking post in the colonies. In the role, he imposed retaliatory actions against the colonists. For example, he convinced Parliament to close the harbor in response to the Boston Tea Party, forcing merchants to pay for the damages.

When he replaced Thomas Hutchinson as Massachusetts's military governor during the onset of the American Revolution, he ordered the redcoats to march toward Concord and Lexington in an attempt to find hidden ammunition and capture the notorious troublemaker Samuel Adams. Of course, Adams managed to escape. But the presence of the British regulars resulted in the pivotal first battle that ultimately kicked off the War of Independence.

"The chaotic skirmishing at Lexington and Concord in April 1775 left the British holed up in Boston and hostile colonists occupying the city's surrounds," wrote Tony Horwitz in the May 2013 edition of *Smithsonian* magazine. "But it remained unclear whether the ill-equipped rebels were willing or able to engage the British Army in pitched battle. Leaders on both sides also thought the conflict might yet be settled without full-scale war."

Gage was caught off guard but convinced that his well-trained British officers could contain the Patriot fighters gathered in Cambridge, Massachusetts. He was wrong. Gage's greatest miscalculation unfolded on June 17, 1775, on Breed's Hill in Charlestown.

"When the rebels opened fire, the close-packed British fell in clumps. In some spots, the British lines became jumbled, making them even easier targets," Horwitz reported. "The Americans added to the chaos by aiming at officers, distinguished by their fine uniforms. The attackers, repulsed at every point, were forced to withdraw."

The British were hit hard, with 1,054 regulars killed or wounded. The Americans had around 400 soldiers down with 115 fatalities. The first true military engagement of the Revolutionary War was considered a Pyrrhic victory in that it inflicted such a devastating toll on the winner that it's basically considered a defeat.

The Battle of Bunker Hill proved to be the military governor's greatest downfall. In a letter to Great Britain's secretary of war, Gage characterized the Patriots as "spirited up by rage and enthusiasm" and finally realized that the rebel fighters were passionate about the cause. "These people show a spirit and conduct against us they never showed against the French," he wrote. "The loss we have sustained is greater than we can bear. Small armies cannot afford such losses, especially when the advantage gained tends to do little more than the gaining of a post."

Three days after authorities received Gage's report from across the pond, he was replaced by General William Howe. The British leader received the order in September and returned to England on October 11, 1775. He returned to his posh family home in London's Portland Place, where died on April 2, 1787, in his late sixties.

What actually sparked the War of Independence? It's up for debate. But if we're looking for the first gunshots fired in retaliation against the redcoats, it wasn't in Lexington or Concord. It was likely in Somerville, Massachusetts.

CONCORD'S COLONIAL INN

Nestled in the heart of historic downtown Concord, the inn sits on land sold to the English settlers by the sachem or Native American tribal chief in 1635. The peaceful transaction happened not far from the property and caused the

According to legend, Dr. Timothy Minot turned his home into a makeshift field hospital to care for wounded soldiers—both colonial militia and British redcoats—during the Battles of Lexington and Concord. *Courtesy of Concord's Colonial Inn.*

new settlers to change the name from the native word "Musketaquid" to "Concord," which is an agreement or harmony between people.

The three-hundred-year-old structure has watched over the town since 1716, witnessed some of the nation's most significant events and hosted some of America's most influential figures. The original builder of the east side of the inn is still a mystery; however, it's known that by the early 1700s, the building was a private residence. Eventually, the home was owned by Colonel James Minot, a justice of the peace, town representative and military colonel. In his time, Minot was the town's wealthiest resident and one of the leaders of the West Congregation, a group of parishioners who separated themselves from the town church for fourteen years in the 1740s and 1750s and held services in the Black Horse Tavern. The tavern stood on the land where the Concord Free Public Library is today.

When Colonel James Minot passed away in 1759, his nephew Dr. Timothy Minot moved into the house, which at the time included only the easternmost side of the property, home to the Thoreau Room.

During Dr. Minot's time, the inn played its most historically significant role. The part of the property that is now home to our front desk and gift shop was built to house weapons and supplies that townsfolk hid in anticipation of an upcoming conflict between the colonists and the King's Army. On April 19, 1775, the Regular Army, or redcoats, used Concord center as their headquarters. They scoured the town, searching for hidden stores of weapons and supplies.

When the Battles of Lexington and Concord were being waged, Dr. Minot's home on the east side of the building served as a hospital where wounded soldiers were cared for. Interestingly, there is no evidence that the British found the supplies hidden in the storehouse.

After the war, Dr. Minot sold his side of the building to his son-in-law Ammi White, a cabinetmaker with a legendary connection to the Revolutionary War. As the redcoats returned across the North Bridge, they saw a fallen soldier with a mangled head. It appeared to the soldiers the man had been scalped. Redcoats reported this horrific sight to their superior officers. In reality, according to the diary of Reverend William Emerson, Ammi White was frightened by a redcoat he thought was dead but then stirred. He struck the dying soldier with his axe. While there was a head injury, there was no scalping. In 1799, Ammi White moved to New Hampshire. He sold the eastern side of the building to an Englishman descended from French Huguenots, Jean Thoreau, Henry David Thoreau's grandfather.

Setting sail from Jersey before his twentieth birthday, Jean Thoreau found himself shipwrecked on the East Coast of the American colonies. He apprenticed with a Boston cooper until the British blocked Boston. As a result of the Siege of Boston, Jean Thoreau became a privateer, which is basically a pirate, under another Boston man descended from French Huguenots, Paul Revere.

After the war, Jean Thoreau became a merchant. He started his business with one hogshead of sugar on Boston's Long Wharf. His business and family grew, and in 1799, Jean Thoreau moved both from Boston to his final home on the eastern side of the Colonial Inn. The main dining room, Merchants Row (the former location of Ammi's cabinet shop), is a nod to Thoreau's nautical profession. After his death, his daughters turned the building into a boardinghouse. The Thoreau sisters' hospitality was well known, and in his writings, Henry David Thoreau fondly remembers visiting his "Aunt's Home" throughout his young adulthood and while studying at Harvard from 1835 to 1837.

The final addition to the historic inn was added sometime between 1812 and 1820 by Deacon White, founder of the Trinitarian Church in Concord. After that, all three sections of the building as they stand today were sold in 1839 to Daniel Shattuck, whose brother Lemuel went on to write one of the earliest histories of the town of Concord. Afterward, in 1889, John Maynard Keyes purchased the two easternmost portions of the inn. He operated them as Thoreau House in honor of the property's past operation as a boardinghouse by Henry David Thoreau's aunts. Subsequently, in 1897, the entire structure was purchased and formally renamed the Colonial Inn.

The building behind the main inn, now known as the Cottage, was initially used as a stable in the late 1800s before being renovated into a home in the early 1900s and used as a boardinghouse. Finally, in 1924, the inn was sold to Mr. Sanborn, who lived in the cottage and called it the "Manager's House." The cottage remained a residence for hotel staff until the 1990s.

The history of Concord's Colonial Inn was written and compiled by the former employees of the inn led by Zachary Trznadel and local historian Beth van Duzer.

PAUL REVERE'S RIDE

Believe it or not, Paul Revere never actually made the trek on horseback to Concord that fateful night. He was captured by British troops one town over in Lincoln. Inspired by Henry Wadsworth Longfellow's poem "Paul Revere's Ride," visitors to the inn often ask about the horse-trotting rabble rouser.

If Revere didn't make it to Concord the night of April 18, 1775, then what really happened?

The famous "one if by land, two if by sea" line from Longfellow's poem is based on actual events orchestrated by Revere and carried out by Old North Church's sexton, or the church's caretaker, Robert Newman. Revere's friend and the church's vestryman Captain John Pulling Jr. was also there to warn the Sons of Liberty that General Thomas Gage and his British troops were coming.

Two lanterns, held that fateful night at the top of Old North Church's wooden steeple, inspired what would become the beginning of the American Revolution.

"Revere enlisted the help of over thirty additional riders. He placed them across the river in Charlestown and ordered the militia leaders to look to the steeple of Old North Church every night for signal lanterns, the number of which indicated when the British army was leaving Boston and by which route," the Old North Foundation explained on its website. "One lit lantern meant the British would march over the Boston Neck, a narrow strip of land and the only road connecting the town to the mainland, which would take a considerable amount of time. Two lit lanterns in the steeple meant the British would take a shortcut by rowing boats across the Charles River into Cambridge, cutting valuable time off their journey."

Newman climbed up the staircases in the back corners of Old North Church and scurried up eight flights of stairs in complete darkness. He lit two lanterns with flint and steel at the top of the steeple and held them for about one minute toward Charlestown, alerting Revere's men, which included the often-overlooked William Dawes.

General Gage, who coincidentally worshiped at Old North Church, was greeted by an armed militia in Lexington. And the rest, as they say, is history.

With such an important role in the days leading up to the American Revolution, it should come as no surprise that one of the nation's most historic churches also brims with the spirits of those who lived and died there during its hundreds of years of tumultuous history. The late Jim McCabe, a noted

The statue of Paul Revere close to the Old North Church commemorates his memorable ride during the American Revolution, although Revere was stopped by British soldiers outside Concord and was unable to finish his famous midnight journey. *Courtesy Deposit Photos.*

ghost lore expert, believed the historic Revolutionary War–era buildings such as Old North Church are ghost magnets. "The old Yankees may have been strange in some ways, but they kept the old buildings, which has made it attractive to many visitors—even ghosts," McCabe told the *Boston Globe*. "Spirits are attracted to places they lived in. I think what attracts ghosts up here is that you don't tear down the buildings."

Built in 1723 by William Prince, Old North is the oldest standing church building in Boston. The famous steeple, which can be seen at various spots throughout Boston and the harbor, fell during Hurricane Carol in 1854. It was fully restored the following year. For the record, it was also blown down by the great gale in 1804 and rebuilt in 1807. And yes, Old North is believed to be haunted.

According to Pam Bennett, retail manager at the popular tourist attraction, the building's former sexton had a close encounter with the misty outlines of three Revolutionary War–era men. "He said they were as clear as day," Bennett told me, adding that the church's sexton was a skeptic and was a bit shocked to run into three full-bodied apparitions at the Salem Street church. "He told them that he's just doing his job, and he noticed their eyes followed him. When he returned, they were gone."

Bennett also mentioned that a woman who lived in the brownstone next to Old North banged on the gift shop door one day and claimed that a boy buried beneath the church regularly visited her North End home. "We told her that we do have unmarked graves beneath the church."

In fact, thirty-seven crypts buried beneath the structure contain the remains of over one thousand former members of Old North Church. But why would a nineteenth-century boy haunt the church's North End neighbor?

Salem Street Academy, a schoolhouse on the north side of the church property, was built in 1810. Boston's first Sunday school got its start at the academy, opening its doors to the city's children in 1815. Co-owned by the church, the Sunday school became popular and welcomed thousands of students, recalled Dr. Charles Downer in his account published in 1893. Henry Ward Beecher, a famous Civil War–era abolitionist, was one of the school's alumni. Beecher's sister Harriet penned the antislavery manifesto *Uncle Tom's Cabin*. The school was replaced by the parish house in 1848 and was officially closed in 1908.

Believe it or not, the woman who had a face-to-face encounter with the ghost boy wearing period garb lives in the exact location that was formerly home to Salem Street Academy. While no reports of untimely deaths at the school in the 1800s can be found, it's common for spirits to return to a place they frequented. "A person doesn't have to die at a location for it to become haunted," wrote Joni Mayhan in *Dark and Scary Things*. "They return because it's a comfortable place for them."

And what about the three Revolutionary War–era spirits spotted by Old North Church's sexton? Mayhan said it's common for ghosts to frequent churches because of guilt over a past deed. "If they feel their sin is great enough, they might balk at crossing over into the light out of fear of where it will bring them," Mayhan continued. "By dwelling at a church, they might feel closer to God and hope to find redemption for their sins."

Of course, hundreds of former parishioners are buried in the labyrinthine crypts in the bowels of Old North Church. While spirits find solace in these places of worship, the emotions associated with important events—like a marriage or even a funeral—can also linger within these hallowed and often historic walls.

Is Revere haunting Old North Church or even his former colonial-era home in Boston's North End? Probably not. The famous minuteman's spirit is rumored to make the rounds near his grave marker at Granary Burying Ground on Tremont Street. In fact, some say his spirit sits on the horse on which he made his famous midnight ride and he continues to guard the hallowed grounds of Boston's third-oldest cemetery in the afterlife.

THE PLAYERS

It was the 250-year anniversary of the Boston Massacre, and I was standing in the middle of a mob of angry protestors gathered outside the Old State House. The chilly March event was supposed to be a re-creation of the pivotal standoff in 1770, but it oddly didn't feel that way. Despite being surrounded by obvious reminders that it's 2020, the vibe seemed like I was actually watching an important historic event unfold. Somehow, I had been transported back in time.

People in the crowds were shouting "go back to England" and "scoundrels," and one overzealous local next to me called the incoming British sentry "lobsters" and "bloody backs." Before the commemoration started, I was told by an actor portraying a wealthy Boston merchant that things were about to get real. "We are trying to be as accurate as possible without actually killing each other," he said with a laugh. Boy, was he right.

As a group of redcoat reenactors fired off their fake flintlock muskets and church bells chimed over the loudspeaker, I tried my best to connect with the spirits of the five murdered colonists using my trusty dowsing rods. No luck. I didn't get a response.

At that moment, however, I did have an epiphany while standing in a sea of frenzied "no taxation without representation" spectators in downtown Boston. Even though it was a reenactment, the mock militiamen were out for blood.

The scene struck a nerve. Reliving the Boston Massacre exactly two and a half centuries later was an eye-opening display of the aggressive male

Built in 1713, the Old State House was the backdrop for the Boston Massacre on March 5, 1770. *Courtesy Deposit Photos.*

psyche gone awry. I've been down this path before. We were celebrating mob violence.

For years, my focus as a paranormal researcher and historian has been on Salem, Massachusetts, and the horrors that unfolded during the witch trials of 1692. As someone who has worked the overnight shift at Concord's Colonial Inn while writing this book, I needed to take an honest look at the lingering energy that has been reported at this notoriously haunted inn.

Joni Mayhan, author of *Ghost Magnet* and *Dark and Scary Things*, believes that the Revolutionary War left an indelible bloodstain on the land and the spirits associated with that initial battle of 1775 couldn't let go of the devastation and injustice.

"War is a violent affair," Mayhan told me. "It changes the vibration of a landscape and alters its energetic composition, leaving it vastly different than it was before the horrors began. Even though many of the souls who fought and died in the battle crossed over and continued their spiritual journeys, many others remained. Some of them didn't realize they were dead, wandering around the battlefields looking for their battalions. Others stayed to look after loved ones or homes they cherished."

Mayhan said that even if the spirits have crossed to a better place, their actions in life likely left a psychic imprint in the area near Concord's Colonial Inn. "As time passed, I believe that many of the earthbound souls eventually found their way to heaven, but the land didn't forget," she said. "The memory of all those lost lives and the devastation of war leached into the ground, leaving a spiritual wound behind."

When asked if she believed the hauntings at the Colonial Inn were more residual or intelligent in nature, Mayhan said it's a layered haunting.

"Residual energy is a memory kept by the land itself," Mayhan explained. "When extreme trauma occurs in an area, it becomes absorbed into the energy field of the location. We know that everything on our planet vibrates. A higher vibration is one that exists harmonically with all that surrounds it. It draws in other high vibrational frequencies, much like metal fragments being pulled to a magnet."

Mayhan said that with most residual hauntings it's an emotional event that is played out over and over again. "A company of soldiers might be spotted in a foggy field, marching out to battle, even though the souls of these soldiers crossed over long ago," she said. "If you tried to communicate with the soldiers, you wouldn't have success, because they aren't really there. What you are seeing is similar to a projection flashed upon a huge screen. It's the memory of a moment caught in time."

Based on Mayhan's research, a location like Concord's Colonial Inn could become more haunted over time because of its proximity to the Old North Bridge. "Places where ghosts are known to linger become almost a waystation for other ghosts who are drawn there by the spiritual energy," she said. "The original haunting was probably focused around the Revolutionary War, but over time, others have joined the colony."

When Mayhan investigated the inn, her team picked up on two spirits in the kitchen that appeared to be more contemporary. "We found a young boy and an older man, neither of whom were tied to the Revolutionary War period," she said.

If Concord's Colonial Inn serves as a "ghost hotel" for many of the spirits lingering in the area, is it possible that the big names from the era actually haunt the inn? For example, multiple guests have reported connecting with Paul Revere at the inn even though he never actually made it to Concord in the wee hours of April 18, 1775. Revere was captured in nearby Lincoln, Massachusetts, by a patrol of British officers who abruptly ended his midnight ride that fateful night but let him go a few hours later without his horse.

I reached out to my friends in the paranormal community asking them why people subconsciously want a recognizable name to explain the hauntings at the Colonial Inn. "Human beings like to label things and make connections," said Richard Estep, a fellow author who has penned several paranormal-themed books on historic locations. "We also love seeing patterns that may not actually be there."

Sarah Streamer, a paranormal researcher who regularly investigates with Estep, echoed her colleague's sentiment. "It's a psychological phenomenon called apophenia," Streamer told me. "Like Richard said, finding connections gives us familiarity. It's hardwired in us. It's how babies come to recognize their mother over a stranger. They make connections. Sometimes we do that for things that aren't there."

Estep believes it's human nature to associate a name with an alleged haunting. "Now that you mention it, there aren't that many cases where investigators admit to not knowing exactly who or what is behind a haunting," he said. "One example where they don't have a name is the Monroe House in Hartford City, Indiana. Nobody's sure whose bones are buried in the crawlspace."

When I mentioned to Estep, who was originally from across the pond, that Paul Revere's name keeps popping up during investigations at Concord's Colonial Inn, he poked fun at the minuteman's famous "the British are coming!" catchphrase. "You'll know if Paul Revere is around if he tells you I'm on the way," Estep said with a laugh, "and if you hear hooves after midnight."

Armed with Estep's idea that "names give us familiarity, and familiarity brings comfort," the following sections shine a light on some of the key figures associated with Concord's Colonial Inn who left their mark throughout the property's illustrious, and sometimes tumultuous, three-hundred-year history.

AMMI WHITE

Out of all the former tenants of what is now Concord's Colonial Inn, the most controversial historical figure who once owned the property on Monument Street is, without question, Ammi White. Before moving into the East House, White participated from the sidelines holding a bloody hatchet during the aftermath of the Battles of Lexington and Concord.

But what actually happened to the then twenty-one-year-old on April 19, 1775, is up for debate. Did White savagely scalp a British soldier in the field next to Old North Bridge, or did he simply put the wounded man out of his misery?

The mystery surrounding White that fateful morning in 1775 isn't an open-and-shut case.

In James H. Stark's "Other Side of the American Revolution" essay, he paints a sympathetic picture of White. According to Stark, "A young man named Ammi White was chopping wood for the Rev. William Emerson" at the Old Manse. During the skirmish at Old North Bridge, White hid under a woodpile and then walked toward the scene of the battle and "saw one British soldier dead, another badly wounded, grasping his ax he struck the wounded soldier on the head crushing in his skull, then taking the soldier's gun he went home."

Stark wrote that White's actions were used as propaganda by the British, and a local newspaper in Boston reported that White had killed one soldier at the bridge with his axe and then savagely mutilated him by cutting off his ears and scalping him. The over-the-top accounts were investigated, and it was revealed that the two redcoats killed by White were buried at the bridge, and neither of them was scalped or disfigured.

In Derek H. Beck's *Igniting the American Revolution*, he negatively portrays White as a bloodthirsty war criminal who "suddenly and swiftly swung his hatchet into the soldier's forehead, instantly dropping the soldier to his

The minuteman statue by Daniel Chester Finch was unveiled at the centennial celebration of the Battles of Lexington and Concord on April 19, 1875. *Courtesy of the Boston Public Library, Print Department.*

knees." According to Beck's account, the Reverend Emerson watched in horror from the Old Manse as White butchered the British soldier. "Ammi White probably smirked at his handiwork—he had just killed himself a redcoat. The murderer then made his escape. How it was possible that not one of the Americans on the overlooking hill saw or acted upon this remains a mystery. Sadly, Ammi White was never punished for his war crime, and secrecy surrounded the shameful incident for decades."

Was White a war criminal with no remorse? Contrary to Beck's take on White, several eyewitnesses to the gruesome ordeal portray White in a less sinister light. Stark cites testimony from Mrs. Peter Barrett that the redcoat killed by White was trying to drown himself in a puddle of water and begged someone to put him out of his misery. The Reverend Emerson kept in contact with White after he moved into what is the eastern side of Concord's Colonial Inn and observed that the man was bothered by the event throughout his life.

Yes, he was haunted by his actions.

When asked if White's murderous backstory somehow left a psychic imprint on Concord's Colonial Inn, former front desk manager Zachary Trznadel said he believes it's definitely possible. "Ammi White is one hell of a dark coincidence to have associated with the building," Trznadel told me. "I don't know much about him outside of the story about the murder at Old North Bridge, and as we know, legends can get out of hand and be more fiction based on little to no fact. I do believe in negative energies, and I think a dark story like his could possibly conjure a negative spirit somehow."

Based on his personal experiences at the inn, Trznadel believes the section of the property formerly inhabited by White is the inn's most haunted. "Guests report having violent dreams in the eastern portion of the inn, and some claim that their beds started to shake uncontrollably," he told me. "I can say without hesitation that room 4 definitely has the strangest vibe, on top of being completely slanted as if it sinks into the ground. In my opinion, that portion of the building is where all of the history lives."

Did White's guilt somehow transform into a manifestation that continues to linger at the inn almost 250 years later? I reached out to my psychotherapist friend Erin Taylor, who is also a paranormal investigator. "Trauma can definitely be a presence of its own," Taylor told me. "Nightmares and beds shaking violently sounds like a trauma response to me. If an individual is having shame, anger or irritability, these things aren't normal. It's possible that an outward manifestation of the man's guilt has taken on a life of its own."

Another possibility is that the trauma followed White to his home and both the perpetrator and victim haunt Concord's Colonial Inn, replaying the murder in an endless ghost loop.

Joni Mayhan believes that locations with ties to heinous crimes have the potential for a residual haunting based purely on their bloody backstories. "I believe that locations of tragic events are more prone to a haunting than any other location," she told me. "When a person dies unexpectedly, sometimes their soul doesn't pass through the white light as it should. The emotions surrounding the event often make them balk. Sometimes when it happens suddenly, they don't even realize they've died. Other times, they remain because of a sense of guilt or a need to let others know what happened to them."

Some locations with ties to crimes, she said, aren't haunted because the victims crossed over to the light. "I once invited my Paranormal 101 class to the murder site of seventeen-year-old Patricia Joyce. She disappeared in 1965 while taking a shortcut through the woods around Crystal Lake in Gardner," Mayhan said. "Her body was found thirty feet from the pumping station. It was the first murder in Gardner in fifty-one years and remains unsolved to this day."

Mayhan's class attempted to reach out to the spirit to help solve the cold case. No luck. "Several of my students are talented psychic-mediums, and none of us were able to connect with Patty's soul. We believe she crossed over immediately, which is sometimes the case. Judging by the information we found in a blog that was written by her sister, Patty was a good girl who typically followed the rules in life. She probably wouldn't have resisted the white light and would have crossed over at the time of her death, like she was supposed to do. The imprint of her death was strong in the area, but we felt it was a residual energy that was absorbed by the location."

Based on this idea that the victims of horrific crimes often cross to the light while the perpetrators stick around because of unfinished business, it's possible that the guilt associated with White's tortured spirit checked into Concord's Colonial Inn more than two centuries ago but never checked out.

DR. TIMOTHY MINOT

All paths seem to lead to Dr. Timothy Minot Jr. when it comes to the legend and lore associated with Concord's Colonial Inn. It was during Minot's ownership of the property that all hell broke loose on April 19, 1775. His role during the skirmish known as the Battles of Lexington and Concord has been the primary point of contention.

Was he the heroic physician, as he is often portrayed, who leaped at the chance to treat the wounded soldiers in a makeshift hospital in his home? And while we're exploring this man of mystery, was he even a surgeon, or has his story been tweaked over time to amplify his importance?

We do know that in the hours leading up to the initial conflict, Minot had a strong hunch that the British were coming. In fact, he was busy escorting his family to a safer location outside the village when the fighting first erupted.

During the American Revolution, Dr. Timothy Minot's property was only a one-story house. The notoriously haunted room is located on the second floor of Concord's Colonial Inn, so it's factually incorrect that room 24 was used as a makeshift surgery room. *Photo by Detroit Publishing Company.*

According to his testimony on April 23, 1775, he was on his way back into town and witnessed the bloodshed unfold near Old North Bridge.

"I had heard of the Regular Troops firing upon Lexington men, and fearing that hostilities might be committed in Concord, thought it my incumbent duty to secure my family," he testified in a sworn statement delivered to the magistrates in Middlesex.

Minot, a 1747 graduate of Harvard College who owned the east side of the structure from 1764 to 1789, testified that the redcoats shot first. "After they fired one gun, then two or three more, before the men that were stationed on the western part of said bridge fired upon them," Minot said under oath.

There was discussion among some of the staff members at the Colonial Inn fueled by research from a local historian that Minot fled Concord with his family and actually hid with them on April 19, 1775. According to the rumor, he supposedly waited until the dust settled so it was safe for the entire family to return home. Based on his sworn testimony in front of several justices of the peace, which included fellow physician John Cuming, he did make the trek back home.

But did he actually triage the wounded at what is now Concord's Colonial Inn?

One of the legends associated with Minot suggested that he used what is now the first-floor dining area, the Liberty Room, as a hospital and one of his bedrooms, now room 24, as an operating room. Room 27 supposedly served as the morgue.

There's a red flag concerning this portion of the story because Minot's home was primarily on the east side of the property. The rooms that supposedly served as Minot's makeshift hospital are on the west side and weren't actually built until 1820. Yes, that's right. The portion of Concord's Colonial Inn considered to be its most haunted didn't exist in 1775.

For years, room 24 has been featured in paranormal-themed books and TV shows as the spot where Minot performed surgery on many of the minutemen wounded in the battle and then kept their corpses in what is now room 27, which is directly beneath the inn's notoriously haunted suite. Not true.

Based on exhaustive research trying to find some facts to support the ghostly encounters reported in those two rooms, there's no way that the western side of the property was used as a makeshift triage area. Room 24 didn't exist in 1775. In fact, the addition was added in the 1800s, and it's not possible that Minot set up shop in this area of the property. But why is the room often cited as the location for Minot's surgery room?

"Most stories like this just become tales that grew in the telling," author Richard Estep from *Haunted Hospitals* told me. "Maybe a former innkeeper wanted to add some spice and color to the inn's reputation, or maybe it was an honest misunderstanding."

Minot, however, did treat wounded soldiers somewhere in what was his home, and it's possible that the savagery associated with eighteenth-century surgery left an indelible mark that somehow migrated and then manifested in room 24. Based on the Stone Tape theory, which suggests that traumatic events can psychically imprint themselves into the environment, it's plausible that the inn's centuries-old wood is stained with the blood of the heroic militia, which resulted in a residual haunting.

But did any of the soldiers from the Battles of Lexington and Concord actually die in Minot's home?

In his book *Lexington and Concord*, Arthur Tourtellot skillfully weaves together a timeline of events. He writes that bloodied soldiers were brought to local physicians around noon on April 19, 1775. "Several of the wounded were taken to Dr. Timothy Minot's in the center of town," he explains, adding that chairs were set up outside Minot's home as an "improvised staff headquarters on the lawn." Tourtellot writes that many of the officers from the battle then gathered at Wright's Tavern. In the early evening, one of Minot's servants dropped off a watch at the local watering hole that had been left at what is now the Colonial Inn.

Minot's property was only one story during the American Revolution, and he had extended his house with a heavily timbered storage space, which is currently the front desk's sitting area. Based on the actual layout of Minot's home, it's possible that he triaged the wounded men in what is now the inn's dining area known as the Liberty Room. Tourtellot writes in *Lexington and Concord* that "some of the more seriously wounded were taken to private houses and quartered in bedrooms." Based on this account, it's highly unlikely that Minot had a makeshift morgue on his property because there's only one death on record that was near his home. The fatality was a British soldier who was being delivered en route from North Bridge. The deceased redcoat was buried in a grave in the center of town. The one casualty with ties to Minot was interred in a spot right across the street from Concord's Colonial Inn. He never made it inside.

According to Louis C. Duncan in *Medical Men in the American Revolution*, "British forces had made little provision for their wounded" because they didn't expect bloodshed. Duncan writes that the serious cases were left where they were shot or stabbed, citing Lieutenant Hall as an example who was wounded and left behind near North Bridge. Hall died the following day.

Based on estimates, there were nearly four hundred soldiers who were either killed, wounded or went missing during the conflict. The British lost seventy-three, and the colonists reported around fifty casualties. According to several accounts, Minot was only responsible for those who weren't seriously wounded. It's possible that he treated a soldier or two who died under his care; however, it wasn't mentioned during his testimony under oath only four days later.

Following the battle, Minot had a successful medical practice in Concord for the remainder of his life and died on August 1, 1804. He was seventy-eight. According to the May 1875 edition of *Harper's Magazine*, he was "one of the most influential founders and supporters of the Middlesex Medical Association." Minot was also praised by his colleagues for dressing the wounds of the minutemen and the British that fateful day in April 1775.

In addition to his heroic dedication to the medical field, Minot's ghost is said to be sticking around his three-hundred-year-old homestead. One of the Colonial Inn's former innkeepers, Loring Grimes, believed the doctor continued to make house calls in the afterlife. When a guest reported seeing a "shadowy mass in the shape of a standing figure" back in June 1968, Grimes told the visitor it could have been the previous owner "merely making his rounds" in what was Minot's home two centuries ago.

My thoughts? I suspect that the shadow figure spotted at Concord's Colonial Inn in the 1960s wasn't Minot but the wounded British soldier who died while being transported from Old North Bridge to the doctor's home in Monument Square. Somehow his specter made his way to the inn, but he didn't have enough energy to fully manifest. The casualty of war is in a perpetual ghost loop and will not be able to cross until he finds some postmortem peace.

HENRY DAVID THOREAU

What was going on in Henry David Thoreau's mind during his time secluded in the cabin immortalized in the book *Walden*?

The nature boy's extensive collection of classical homoerotic literature and his blatant affection for a certain Walden Pond visitor and Canadian woodchopper, Alek Therien, suggested a secret yearning to live his life authentically.

What does Thoreau's orientation have to do with it? If he was struggling with the anxiety and guilt associated with sexual desire up until his death on May 6, 1862, then it's possible that his internal conflict would continue in the afterlife.

But if Thoreau's ghost is still sticking around, where is he? The obvious choice would be the iconic cabin in the woods. However, as *Storied Waters* author David A. Van Wie mused online in his essay "Chasing Thoreau's Ghost," he's probably not hanging out at his former haunt.

"As much as he enjoyed living 'deliberately' in a one room, rustic cabin, would Henry want to hole-up there for the next one-hundred-and-fifty years? The cabin no longer exists, although archaeologists eventually found the footings of the chimney," Van Wie wrote. "They have a cabin replica at the Walden Pond Reservation, but I doubt very much his ghost would be there. Maybe a replica ghost?"

Van Wie's quest to find the famed transcendentalist's spirit led him to the Concord River. In his book *A Week on the Concord and Merrimack Rivers*, Thoreau journeyed with his brother John, who died of tetanus only three

The Thoreau Room function area at Concord's Colonial Inn is located in the eastern side of the property and is where Henry David Thoreau's aunts likely welcomed guests to their boardinghouse. *Courtesy of Concord's Colonial Inn.*

years after the adventure in 1839. Thoreau wrote *A Week*, in part, as a tribute to his brother's memory.

"John's death deeply affected Henry, so the book was very important to him. He wrote the first draft of *A Week* while living at Walden Pond, and it was published five years before *Walden*," Van Wie wrote. "My guess is that, if I were to encounter Henry's ghost, it would be on the Concord River, paddling with John on an eternal, joyful outing, there on the waters close to home."

While Van Wie's theory is a good one, I would suggest Concord's Colonial Inn as a possible postmortem hangout for the ghost of Thoreau. He stayed in the building when he attended Harvard from 1835 to 1837. Also, the boutique hotel was renamed the Thoreau House after Henry's aunts, the "Thoreau Girls," in the mid-1800s.

There's even a resident spirit at Concord's Colonial Inn that fits Thoreau's description. "Room 24, which is in the oldest part of the inn, is reportedly haunted," Peter Muise posted in "Concord's Haunted Inn" on his website, New England Folklore. A man wearing old-school clothing has been seen repeatedly in that room. "He never harms anyone or speaks, but simply walks toward the fireplace and disappears," Muise wrote.

Judith Fellenz, from Highland Falls, New York, had a similar encounter in room 24 back in 1966. "As I opened my eyes, I saw a grayish figure at the side of my bed, to the left, about four feet away," Fellenz recalled. "It was not a distinct person but a shadowy mass in the shape of a standing figure. It remained still for a moment, then slowly floated to the foot of the bed, in front of the fireplace. After pausing a few seconds, the apparition slowly melted away. It was a terrifying experience. I was so frightened I could not scream."

There's even a story from Thomas D'Agostino in *Haunted New England* about a group of paranormal investigators who checked out the paranormally active room in 2005. Members of the team saw a full-bodied apparition of a man wearing 1800s-era attire. And, get this, the ghost threw a book at the investigators.

D'Agostino and his partner Arlene Nicholson recently reconvened at the inn for their "Dining with the Dead 1031" event to investigate on the anniversary of Thoreau's passing on May 6, 1862. While they didn't necessarily connect with the *Walden* author's spirit, Nicholson told me that Thoreau left an indelible mark on the property. "We investigated what was called the Thoreau Room in the past, and I definitely kept picking up creativity using my tarot cards," she said. "I would say Henry David Thoreau possibly left a psychic imprint on that side of the property."

A few weeks before the "Dining with the Dead" investigation, a long-term guest who was staying in the Thoreau section of the house said he spotted a writing pen fling across the room one morning. "I'm a skeptic when it comes to ghosts, but I clearly saw the writing pen shoot across the table."

When I mentioned that it's believed that Henry David Thoreau stayed in what is now room 4 while he was a student at Harvard, the guest (who preferred to remain anonymous) nodded his head. "It makes sense," he said. "I just turned on the TV, and it felt like whatever was in the room wanted me to make the noise stop."

If Thoreau's ghost is still lingering at Concord's Colonial Inn, he's likely hanging out in his old room in the eastern section of the property and not in room 24. If you do want to commune with the spirit of the *Walden* author, don't turn on the television, or his lingering energy may literally throw the book at you.

THE HAUNTINGS

Why is Concord so haunted? Richard Estep, a paranormal-themed author originally from the United Kingdom who is currently based in Colorado, believes there's an indelible scar associated with the "shot heard 'round the world" that has psychically imprinted itself into the land. "The more blood-soaked the ground, the more haunted it tends to be," Estep told me. "Battlefields and ghosts tend to go hand in hand."

Estep said that the American Revolution's first campaigns in Lexington and Concord were particularly brutal engagements. "The colonials were fighting for their freedom and defending their home turf," he said. "Their opponent was the greatest military machine in the world at the time, the British army. Redcoats were trained to fire disciplined volleys in rapid succession. They caused carnage on the battlefield. That's a lot of death and injury in a relatively short amount of time."

The paranormal investigator—who has been featured on Travel Channel shows like *Haunted Case Files*, *A Haunting* and *Paranormal Nightshift*—said that the reenactors who gather at the original battle's location somehow stir the paranormal pot. "Reenactment is essentially simulation, and in my experience, appropriately simulating events that have taken place at a haunted location can sometimes act as a catalyst for further paranormal activity."

Estep believes that "wherever one finds very strong emotion, one tends to find ghosts. Battlefields are the epitome of strong emotion, most often terror, rage, regret and pain. That makes for a very potent mixture of energy, which, some theorize, spirit entities may be able to derive power in order to manifest."

Rooms 24 and 27 are said to be the inn's most haunted, but the ghosts aren't confined to one area and reportedly like to wander the halls. *Courtesy of the Boston Public Library, Print Department.*

Armed with the idea that there's a lingering energy associated with the battle that ignited the American Revolution, Estep said it's likely that activity in Concord intensifies in April. "Anniversary hauntings are well documented," he insisted. "Based on anecdotal evidence, activity in and around Gettysburg, for example, tends to pick up as July approaches each year."

As far as the type of hauntings associated with the Battles of Lexington and Concord, Estep told me that the ghosts he has encountered at similar battlefield sites are predominantly residual in nature, and their imprints will likely fade over time. "The more people experience them, the more they tend to diminish in strength, as if it's a battery slowly being run down to exhaustion with each successive paranormal experience," he explained.

Estep said it makes sense if some of the residual energy associated with the conflict at Old North Bridge may have redirected itself to the Colonial Inn, especially "if any of the dead or wounded were brought there afterward," he said.

Speaking of well-known destinations with ties to war, the prolific author who got his start as a paranormal investigator has written about this phenomenon before with other locations that are near haunted battlefields. In fact, Estep seems to naturally gravitate toward properties—like the Farnsworth House Inn in Gettysburg or Fort Mifflin in Philadelphia—that have ties to major battles, "As my writing career progresses, I enjoy devoting an entire book to a single location," he said. "It feels as though the story has more room to breathe over the space of fifty thousand words than it does when it's compressed into a single chapter. I have become very fond of some of the locations I investigate and like to delve into the lives of those who lived and worked there."

For his single-location books, Estep usually writes the first section at the haunted location he is featuring. "I feel that it helps capture the atmosphere of the place in some small way," he explained. "Each book, or chapter of a book, is a reminder of that time of my life and takes me right back there when I open up the book months or years later. I hope to one day be an old man who can go to the bookshelf in order to relive some of the high points of my life."

Estep also said it's important to him as an author and investigator to completely immerse himself at the haunted locations he writes about, especially for his single-location books.

"I love the storytelling process, and that begins with the research and the 'boots on the ground' component of paranormal investigation," he said. "It's one thing to tell ghost stories that you've gotten from interviewing witnesses. It's another thing entirely to spend a week living, sleeping and investigating in the place that you're writing about. I think it adds credibility."

Similar to Estep, Brian J. Cano from *Paranormal Caught on Camera* and *The Haunted Collector* was a longtime paranormal investigator before penning his first book, *Grains of Sand: Tales of a Paranormal Life*.

According to Cano when I interviewed him for my *Ghosts of the American Revolution* book, the playback hauntings Estep alluded to can be exacerbated by the living. "We're constantly expending energy and leaving bits of ourselves behind," Cano said. "These sorts of things are the basic building blocks of an echo."

When Revolutionary War performers replay the Battles of Lexington and Concord every April, Cano believes it could stir up the sleepy spirits. "Reenactors are very dedicated to their performances," he said. "When they're in uniform, they are out for blood, and that energy can be left behind. The battle is replayed over and over again, and I believe the spirits are reenergized because of it."

Cano echoes Estep's belief that the ghosts of Concord's bloodstained past will diminish over time. "As we go on in time, the ghosts from the Revolutionary War will dissipate, and we'll start talking to ghosts from the twentieth century," he told me. "As we move forward in our timeline, the energy also moves forward."

When it comes to spirit communication with the original ghosts of Concord's Colonial Inn, Cano isn't convinced they're still sticking around. "The minute you start investigating, you're sending a signal to the astral plane that you're attempting to make contact with the spirit realm," he said. "When we send out that signal, you never know who or what is responding."

If investigators claim that they're communicating with the more well-known ghosts associated with the American Revolution, Cano said that it may be wishful thinking. "If someone is trying to contact George Washington and they get a response, they're going to automatically think it's him," he said. "How would they know what George Washington sounded like? There's no logic behind that approach. People try to connect the dots too quickly."

As someone who shares a birthday with America's first president, Cano said Washington probably powered through most of his legendary career and doesn't want to revisit the bloodstained battlefields he once overlooked. "He didn't want to do half of the things that he did during his lifetime, but he did it because it was required of him. He did it out of service," Cano said. "He put one foot in front of the other and kept walking. He had no inkling that there would be monuments honoring him one day or that he would be on the one-dollar bill."

When it comes to the founding fathers, Cano said that we put them on pedestals, but they were regular people who happened to win the battle for independence and probably wouldn't want to relive the day-to-day stresses of creating a new nation.

"War is hell," he said. "It wasn't a great time, and I couldn't imagine any of the people living it felt like they were going to be celebrated in the future. When people look back at events like the American Revolution, what actually took place is probably very different from the romanticized story that we now commemorate."

GHOSTLY GUESTS

When travelers check into Concord's Colonial Inn and ask about the ghosts, they're handed a document outlining the various paranormal reports

Guests who stay at Concord's Colonial Inn feel like they step back in time thanks to historical details like the old-school key system and mail slots located behind the front desk. *Photo by Sam Baltrusis.*

collected over the years from guests. The list includes an older woman and a tall, slim gentleman wearing a top hat spotted in the sitting room. There are also multiple accounts of Revolutionary War–era soldiers and even a playful little girl who wears a bonnet.

Zachary Trznadel, a former manager who eventually became the go-to guy regarding the inn's hauntings, told me he didn't believe the ghostly hype until he started working at the front desk.

"Growing up Roman Catholic, we were taught to stay as far away from that stuff as possible, so the building totally opened me up," he told me. "As a staff member, you're quickly indoctrinated with the history of the building and its ghosts."

Trznadel told me that he didn't give the paranormal much thought until he had a face-to-face encounter with a female spirit when he first started working at the inn. "It was during the evening shift, and I felt something watching me," he recalled. "I was standing at the computer to the left, and the lamp was partially obstructing my view into the sitting room. I looked out of the corner of my eye and thought I saw a figure. I then looked again in the direction and saw a woman who was almost a shade of gray and had salt-and-pepper hair. She was wearing a hat and was staring straight at me. I don't know how to explain it other than it caught my eye, and then she disappeared. I remember thinking I was crazy, and I wanted to quit for about two weeks after that night."

The longtime front desk employee said he tried to shrug off the encounter until he chatted with a couple who stayed in a supposedly not haunted room in the main inn. "They came downstairs, and the boyfriend had seen someone and asked if there was anything tied to room 20. I told him no," Trznadel said. "He then described this woman in a dress and hat with salt-and-pepper hair. It totally hit me that this woman exists."

Trznadel said his only regret was that he wished he wasn't so scared.

"I told her to 'stay there' and to not follow me home," he remembered. "I said I never wanted to see her again, and I actually didn't after that night. I honestly regret saying that to her."

In addition to the middle-aged woman haunting the inn, there are also sightings of a young girl wearing a bonnet who has been seen walking around by the front desk of the hotel. She's believed to be the one responsible when items fall off the shelves or go missing without a trace and then mysteriously pop up again.

Trznadel said that he's heard multiple accounts of the little girl who allegedly haunts the inn. "One of the long-term maintenance workers and probably the most honest person I know said there was a girl running back and forth between rooms 22 and 24," Trznadel told me. "He swears by it."

The maintenance worker said the spirit looked around six or seven years old. "It was a shadow, but you could clearly see it was a child," he told Trznadel.

According to the former front desk manager, there's a backstory to the girl who supposedly died at the inn, but he believes it's more legend than fact. "It's said that room 22 was home to this little girl, and she had gotten really sick and supposedly passed away," he said. "Apparently a medium had come in and said her name was Josephine and found her grave in Sleepy Hollow Cemetery, but I've never gone to great lengths to figure that out."

While managing the front desk staff, Trznadel said he heard all sorts of things like lights flickering in guests' rooms and then turning off completely. There were reports of disembodied whispers coming from empty rooms, and some guests have seen an apparition of what appeared to be a wounded soldier.

Trznadel said the former housekeeping manager was cleaning a mirror in the Heritage Room downstairs when she felt like someone was tugging on

Zachary Trznadel, the former front desk manager, spotted a ghostly woman sitting in the parlor area of Concord's Colonial Inn. *Photo by Sam Baltrusis.*

her shirt even though she was alone. She didn't say anything until another employee experienced the same exact thing. Other staff members said they were touched from behind and turned around expecting to find a child trying to get their attention, but there was no one there.

Reports run the gamut, including glasses clinking in celebration way past last call to items levitating in the gift shop area and then being slung across the room. Both guests and employees report seeing spirits wearing colonial attire sitting in an otherwise empty dining area called the Liberty Room.

"War sites are always notorious for having lots of spiritual activity. Gettysburg is another similar haunted location. Where tragedy occurs, so will legends," Trznadel said. "I emphasize the word *legend* because it plays a huge role in the story of Concord's Colonial Inn. The building is so haunted because of its legendary status."

Trznadel believes that paranormal investigators flock to the inn because of the ghost stories, and by trying to communicate with the dead, they somehow stir up the activity. "It's the right people trying to contact the wrong entities," he said, adding that the endless investigations have upset the spirits while simultaneously giving them more energy to manifest.

When asked what's the greatest hurdle he encountered while working at Concord's Colonial Inn, Trznadel said it's the attempt to separate fact from fiction. "Trying to uncover the truth is a huge challenge because the place and its ghosts are well known," he said. "Do I think the inn is haunted? Yes. But I also think a large percentage of the stories I've heard over the years are more wishful thinking and less about actual experiences with the inn's ghosts."

HAUNTED ROOMS

Room with a boo? Based on firsthand accounts and local legends, Concord's Colonial Inn has two of them. Rooms 24 and 27 are said to be the inn's most haunted.

The legend is retold in a leaflet handed out to ghost-hunting guests, stating that the inn's "most famous, haunted, and sought-after guest room is Room 24." The story told in the "Ghosts of Concord's Colonial Inn" handout reports that the "right side of the inn was privately owned by Dr. Timothy Minot" and the Liberty Room dining area on the first floor served as a makeshift hospital during the Battles of Lexington and Concord. In the written story, room 24 was said to be Minot's operating room. The handout also states that "the deceased were carried directly downstairs into Room 27, which was used as a morgue."

Zachary Trznadel, the inn's former front desk manager, told me that information employees hand out to guests is historically inaccurate.

"The legend of room 24 has been around for ages, but the story of room 27 is somewhat new," Trznadel said, adding that the dark history associated with room 27 is only a few decades old. "There weren't always two haunted rooms," he said. "The story has been manufactured over time."

Trznadel confirmed that the section of the inn where rooms 24 are 27 are located wasn't actually built in the eighteenth century. "Not only was the room nonexistent in the 1700s, it most certainly wasn't a morgue," he said. "To avoid disease and the smell of rotting flesh, dead bodies were put outside or in basements where plenty of fresh air could come in. Morgues didn't become a thing until the 1860s which was almost a century after Dr. Minot owned the property."

Sadly, the stories told online and in countless periodicals are not historically correct.

"We need to talk about what we know and separate fact from fiction," Trznadel said. "Based on historical research, rooms 24 and 27 were not

Guests have reported paranormal activity in room 24 since the 1960s and claim to see ghostly shadows or Revolutionary War soldiers standing at the foot of their bed. *Courtesy of Concord's Colonial Inn.*

present when Dr. Timothy Minot was around. Period. The stories of a makeshift Revolutionary War hospital didn't happen in those two rooms."

However, Minot did have a first-floor extension on the western side of the property in 1775, and it's possible that what is now the Liberty restaurant area was used to treat both militiamen and British soldiers on April 19, 1775. While the inn's most haunted rooms don't necessarily have a bloody backstory, Trznadel told me that he strongly believes that the western side of the Colonial Inn is indeed haunted. "Guests absolutely have experiences in those two rooms," he said. "I don't believe in hauntings at Concord's Colonial Inn being tied down to certain rooms. It's property wide."

If rooms 24 and 27 didn't exist in 1775, then why all of the paranormal activity? Based on firsthand reports, the accounts seem to have intensified.

Sean Austin, a demonologist who was the lead investigator on the Travel Channel's *Ghost Loop*, told me on my *Haunted Hotels* podcast that he had one helluva night when he stayed in room 24. "We just had so much activity in that room, it was unbelievable," he said. "It's definitely in the top five when it comes to haunted hotels that I've stayed at for sure."

Austin explained that he picked up on the residual energy that manifested as panic and chest pains in room 24. "It was hard to breathe in that room," he said. "There was this crazy light anomaly that kept coming out of the bathroom area. We even captured it on video. There were a lot of references to the hospital and the injuries sustained by the soldiers that we validated on our investigation equipment."

The paranormal investigator said he felt an intense energy circling around the room during his stay in 2020. "There was endless communication through our EMF detector, and the MEL meter kept going off. And then there was a stick figure using the SLS camera. There was just so much going on. It's interesting, when you stay in a small room at a hotel, but there's such a profound psychic imprint in that room, it's like history is still alive in that inn."

When asked if the activity in room 24 was residual or intelligent in nature, Austin said it was a combination of both. "The panic feeling I was picking up on was definitely residual energy from the soldier not knowing if they are going to live or die. As paranormal researchers, we know it leaves a stain on the land forever. It stains the land. It stains the area. However, there were definitely intelligent souls communicating with us too."

Based on his spirited stay at Concord's Colonial Inn, Austin suggested that there may be a portal in the room that allows for spirits to come and go as they please.

Thomas D'Agostino and Arlene Nicholson frequent the inn and have investigated both rooms 24 and 27 during the "Dining with the Dead 1031" events. Similar to Austin's analysis, D'Agostino believes that the hauntings at Concord's Colonial Inn are multilayered. "It could be residual or intelligent and they're stuck in an energy pocket which causes them to remain," D'Agostino told me on my *Haunted Hotels* podcast. "Or, they could just love it so much at the Colonial that they don't want to leave. The Thoreau family lived there. There were many people who lived there, and they loved it."

D'Agostino continued, "The history alone is amazing, but when you add the hauntings it's even more fascinating."

Nicholson said one couple who stayed in room 27 had a profound experience during an overnight event organized by their "Dining with the Dead 1031" team. "A couple from our group stayed in that room after the investigation. and they were so excited to tell us what happened to them in Room 27," Nicholson recalled. "The couple was getting ready to go to sleep. As the husband was closing his eyes, he felt a gentle touch on his arm. He automatically thought it was his wife. He looked over at her and she was at the other side of the huge king-size bed. He thought it was strange but eventually went to sleep."

As the evening progressed, the experience turned darker for the couple. "A few hours later, he was awoken three times during the night with a jabbing sensation that he could only describe [as] what felt like a bullet in the back of his shoulder. The feeling would jerk him awake," Nicholson said. "Although he felt no pain, I believe he was almost tapping into the spirit of one of the wounded soldiers kept in that room. At around 3:30 a.m., the couple both woke to the sound of knocking on the closet door, which happened a few times throughout the night."

As Trznadel pointed out previously, both rooms 24 and 27 didn't exist in 1775, so what's really going on? Over the years, the former front desk manager has seen all sorts of things, including what looked like a pentagram etched into the carpet of room 24, and witnessed freaked-out guests who strongly believed they were attacked by an unseen force in one of the so-called haunted rooms. "In my opinion, it's potentially dangerous," Trznadel told me. "If someone is speaking to a soldier or doctor in room 24, they're talking to a spirit presenting themselves as such, and that's a problem."

Trznadel told me that he worried about dark entities impersonating wounded soldiers and feeding off of the fear perpetuated by thrill-seekers. "Investigators spend a lot of time believing the story of the spirits in rooms 24 and 27 supposedly being from a Revolutionary War–era hospital. People eat it up," Trznadel said. "From my perspective, it's all a dangerous trap."

While it's historical fact that the two rooms pinpointed as the inn's most haunted weren't actually built until the 1800s, Trznadel does think it's possible that some ghosts haunting Concord's Colonial Inn stop by rooms 24 and 27 because that's where they get the most attention. "The biggest question for me isn't if Concord's Colonial Inn is haunted, it's who or what is haunting the property," he said. "There's definitely someone or something there."

Is it a wounded soldier or Dr. Timothy Minot? Trznadel isn't convinced. "Legends can get out of hand and fiction can become fact if the stories are told over and over. I do believe in negative energies, and focusing on the darker side of the inn's history—even if it's not based on actual fact—can somehow manifest a negative entity by the people who believe the story and present historical inaccuracies as fact."

TV INVESTIGATIONS

Concord's Colonial Inn has been featured in several paranormal-themed TV shows over the years. This culminated with a visit from TAPS (The Atlantic Paranormal Society) in an episode of Syfy's *Ghost Hunters* called "A Shot in the Dark" that premiered on September 15, 2010.

What's interesting about the televised investigation led by Jason Hawes and Grant Wilson is that they discussed in detail the genesis of the ghost lore associated with the inn, which started with a paranormal encounter in room 24.

"In the 1960s, there was a woman who stayed there who had an experience and it actually got published," reported case manager Kris Williams. "Since then, the place has been known as a haunted spot. There have been several deaths there, but they are not sure of the numbers. They believe that's where the activity is coming from, and they are trying to figure out who would be hanging around there."

Before making the trek from Warwick, Rhode Island, to Concord, Wilson discussed the idea that the actual history associated with the inn could have been twisted over time. "The Colonial has been around for three-hundred-plus years," Wilson said on the TV show. "Legends can turn into fact and then become reality. There's a lot of history and a lot of reports, so I'm eager to get in there and help the inn decide if this place has got activity or not."

The team from the original *Ghost Hunters* TV show investigated Concord's Colonial Inn in 2010 and checked out Merchants Row, where a ghostly woman wearing a navy blue dress was spotted sitting at one of the restaurant's tables. *Courtesy of Concord's Colonial Inn.*

When the team arrived, they met in the front desk area and were led throughout the inn by former front desk employee Arthur Martin. "This was part of the original structure in 1716," Miller told Hawes and Wilson. "It was a provincial storage house and a general store. What makes this spot special to our country is on April 19, 1775, the wounded were brought in here from Old North Bridge."

Martin talked about the paranormal experiences employees have reported while working in the lobby, which included items being thrown off the shelf and inexplicable power surges. "Someone will say something, and all of a sudden the lights will go out, and they will say something else and the lights will go back on," Martin said. "It's almost as if the lights are responding to what people are saying."

He then walked the TAPS team to the Liberty Room, which is the dining area right behind the front desk. "This is where many of the dying men were brought from the battle at Old North Bridge," Martin explained. "People have reported being touched on the shoulder, and others report having strange feelings in the Liberty Room. There is one report of a gentleman with a top hat sitting at one of the tables."

When Wilson asked where the figure was spotted in the Liberty Room, Miller said it was "seen in the mirror of all places. They were looking, and the image appeared in the mirror."

In Merchants Row, there was a woman sitting at one of the tables wearing an old-fashioned navy blue dress with ruffles on the skirt. Upstairs in the hallway next to room 24, Miller said that guests have reported hearing phantom footsteps go up and down the stairs throughout the night and items in their rooms would go missing and then suddenly reappear. One guess swore she saw a full-bodied apparition of "a woman descending down the stairs and wearing a period dress," Martin recalled, adding that the apparition was see-through but clearly had an outline to it.

During the tour of room 24, Martin said there were reports of two bloodied soldiers wearing full Revolutionary War gear standing at the foot of the bed, and the door would open and close without anyone turning the knob.

Hawes and Wilson had an unusually active investigation at the inn, with the most convincing evidence involving the door in room 24. The duo investigating the room asked if the spirits could make their presence known, and the door suddenly closed. They then told the spirits of room 24 that if they would close the door again, they would pack up their equipment and leave them alone. The door slammed shut, and the team left the room out of respect.

Jason Hawes and Grant Wilson from the TV show *Ghost Hunters* investigated reports of a gentleman spirit wearing a top hat seen in the Liberty Room restaurant. *Courtesy of Concord's Colonial Inn.*

Zachary Trznadel, Concord's Colonial Inn's former front desk manager, told me that the visit from *Ghost Hunters* was a double-edged sword. "The show shined a national spotlight on the inn's ghosts," Trznadel said, adding that if you type in "haunted hotel" in an online search engine more than a decade later, Concord's Colonial Inn is one of the top results. "Haunted tourism works," he said. Trznadel also believes the attention from the show seemed to "make the spirits angry but has brought them more to life."

Since the show aired, Trznadel said hundreds of paranormal enthusiasts have booked room 24. He also said that some of the more seasoned investigators try to debunk the evidence from TAPS and point out that there's a spring on the haunted room's door, which would explain the dramatic opening and closing during the televised investigation.

Trznadel said that some of the activity reported by Martin in the *Ghost Hunters* episode continues to be relevant today, including strange power surges in the lobby that seem to respond on command and the lady wearing the blue period dress, who has been spotted by several guests. In fact, Trznadel has even seen her in the sitting room area near the front desk.

Speaking of the ghostly woman haunting Concord's Colonial Inn, psychic-medium Chris Fleming, who was the lead for the second season of *Psychic Kids: Children of the Paranormal*, told me that he spotted an apparition while filming the show in 2009.

During the investigation conducted by the team from *Ghost Hunters*, the door of room 24 mysteriously slammed shut and was cited as possible paranormal activity, even though it was later debunked. *Courtesy of Concord's Colonial Inn.*

"When we were shooting the episode of *Psychic Kids* near the stairs, we caught a glimpse of the lower torso of a woman in white walking up the stairs," Fleming recalled. "We raced after it and it was completely gone, it was solid. Unfortunately, I think they left it out of the final cut of the episode."

Fleming also confirmed Martin's comments on *Ghost Hunters* that objects mysteriously disappear and then reappear in some of the main inn's rooms. "The one thing that struck me was when I arrived, I went up to my hotel room to shower, and I used to wear an ancient runes charm around my neck," Fleming told me. "I took the pendant off, put it on top of the dresser and got into the shower. As soon as I got out of the shower, I went to reach for the necklace to put it back on my neck, but it was gone."

More than a decade after *Ghost Hunters* filmed at Concord's Colonial Inn, the paranormal activity reported to TAPS seems to be consistent with the supernatural shenanigans still happening today. Looking to sleep with spirits validated by the paranormal pop culture's top investigators? Check into one of the main inn's rooms for the ultimate dead inn experience.

THE LEGENDS

When I was interviewed by local talk show host Bradley Jay in October 2019, I was able to solve a mystery that has haunted the WBZ radio personality for years: *Who was Black Mark?*

Jay had asked other local authors and historians on his late-night podcast, and they had no clue what he was talking about. "I heard indirectly that there was a man who was hanged in Boston Common and was laid there to rot for four years," he said. "All I remembered was that his name was Black Mark."

While the location of Jay's story was incorrect, Mark's tragic backstory was shockingly true.

"It was horrific," I said on the live broadcast of his *Jay Talking* radio show. "This was in 1755, years after the Salem witch trials, and Mark wasn't hanged in Boston but in Cambridge of all places. Mark was accused of murdering a slave owner along with a woman named Phillis. They took his body and put it into a gibbet cage, which was a crude contraption designed by the Puritans as a public reminder of his crime."

During the eighteenth century, the case was well known. In fact, Paul Revere mentioned Mark in the account of his famous midnight ride on April 18, 1775. The enslaved duo and supposed co-conspirators, however, were somehow forgotten by history.

"It's surprising to me that we don't talk about this story because it's such a horrible way to execute someone," I said on the radio show. "What is even more tragic is that Mark and Phillis were probably innocent of killing Captain Codman. They were scapegoats in my opinion."

The equestrian statue of George Washington is located in Boston's Public Garden. *Courtesy Deposit Photos.*

I first heard about the tragic story when I interviewed Gavis Kleespies, former director of the Cambridge Historical Society, in 2013.

"Mark and Phillis, two slaves accused of poisoning Captain John Codman, a Charlestown merchant whose 'rigid discipline' they had found 'unendurable,' were executed," Kleespies recounted in the historical society's newsletter. "Phillis, as was customary, was strangled and her body burned. Mark was hanged and his body suspended in irons on a gibbet along what is now Washington Street in Somerville, near the Charlestown line."

When Paul Revere rode past the gibbet cage twenty years after the hanging, Mark's decomposed body became a literal landmark for the minuteman. "After I had passed Charlestown Neck, and got nearly opposite where Mark was hung in chains, I saw two men on horseback, under a tree," Revere recalled. "When I got near them, I discovered they were British officers."

Mark was hanged in Cambridge and then tarred and gibbeted in an iron cage near the present-day Holiday Inn on Somerville's Washington Street. According to one unnamed colonial-era physician, the tar used to preserve the body had surprisingly worked, and the doctor wrote that Mark's "skin was but a little broken altho' he had been hanging there for nearly three or four years."

Apparently, the "Black Mark" moniker wasn't referring to the color of the executed man's skin but the black tar used to keep his corpse intact. Phillis, on the other hand, was savagely strangled and then burned at the stake.

And yes, this tragedy has psychically imprinted itself in the environment.

According to local sources, many of the homes and former Lesley College buildings surrounding the execution site are teeming with the tortured spirits from Cambridge's Gallows Hill past.

"Phenomena include disembodied footsteps and objects that move by themselves," wrote Dennis William Hauck in *Haunted Places: The National Directory*. Also, the *Boston Globe* reported that Phillis's cries can be heard echoing throughout Avon Hill. "They say, if you listen closely on a windy day, you can still hear her screaming as she went up in smoke," said tour guide Daniel Berger-Jones.

Is it Phillis posthumously begging for justice and setting the record straight about the man she and Mark may—or may not—have murdered with arsenic?

While researching the Mark and Phillis case in 2013, I was mysteriously drawn to the oldest structure in Cambridge, the Cooper-Frost-Austin House on Linnaean Street. It's open once a year, in June, and my intuition led me to the little white building tucked away in North Cambridge's Avon Hill. The lean-to "half house" was built by Samuel Cooper, a deacon of First Church, in the early eighteenth century and was passed down the Cooper family tree for 250 years. The historic home is a stone's throw from Cambridge's Gallows Hill. And, yes, that's the spot where Mark and Phillis were executed.

While dozens of people were hanged near the property during the colonial era, the spirit haunting the Cooper-Frost-Austin House passed in 1885. According to Brian Powell, the structure's year-round resident and tour guide, he's heard several stories from former tenants who claim the ghost of the last owner, Susan Austin, still lingers in the upstairs bedroom.

"I was checking out a book at the Boston Public Library, and the librarian recognized my address as the Cooper-Frost-Austin House. He said that he lived here for a week and would never go back," Powell told me.

Why? "He said it was haunted. He was literally spooked and spent a week in this house in complete terror. People speculate it's the last owner, Susan Austin, but I've never encountered her," Powell said, joking that he's comfortable sharing a home with the female specter. "I don't care if she's here. You can be dead as long as you don't bother me when I'm sleeping," he said. "But I've been approached by psychics and others who believe the house is active."

As far as my baseline sweep of the oldest building in Cambridge, I did spot what looked like a shadow figure dart across the downstairs in the main hall, which boasts original masonry detail in the fireplaces and the foot of the structure's chimney dating back to 1681.

During the tour, a hanging lamp mysteriously started to sway when we were in the original kitchen area, and when our small group toured the haunted upstairs bedroom, eerily in a state of arrested decay, we heard inexplicable phantom footsteps creaking above us in the attic. Apparently, the third floor is where the servants stayed. In the past, I've spotted what looked like a full-bodied apparition of a woman, lit by candlelight, peeking from the window of the second-floor bedroom when I walked down Linnaean Street.

The weekend before my visit to the Cooper-Lee-Nichols House, I was asked a question while giving one of my ghost tours that really baffled me: Why were all of the spirits featured on my historical-based ghost tours in Boston mostly "white men with money"?

I was stumped. I couldn't think of one story during our walk through Boston's haunted cemeteries and cobblestone streets that featured a person of color. The question inspired me to dig a little deeper for the skeletal secrets hidden in the city's Revolutionary War–era closet.

"By 1775, more than a half million African Americans, most of them enslaved, were living in the thirteen colonies," wrote historian Edward Ayres on the American Revolution Museum at Yorktown's website. "Widespread talk of liberty gave thousands of slaves high expectations, and many were ready to fight for a democratic revolution that might offer them freedom. In 1775 at least ten to fifteen black soldiers, including some slaves, fought against the British at the battles of Lexington and Bunker Hill. By 1776, however, it had become clear that the revolutionary rhetoric of the founding fathers did not include enslaved blacks."

In the early drafts of the Declaration of Independence, for example, Thomas Jefferson changed the semantics from "all men are born equally free" to "all men were created equal" to prevent the idea that enslaved men and women should be free.

Yes, human trafficking was a hot-button topic in the years leading up to the American Revolution, and the subject would rear its ugly head during the Civil War less than one century later.

In 1772, the British courts issued a landmark court decision that involved a runaway slave, James Somerset, who fled his owner Charles Stewart in Boston. The abolitionist movement overseas sided with the enslaved man in the *Somerset v. Stewart* case, and the courts decided that "slavery was antithetical to the British constitution and English common law." This ruling wasn't enforced in America, and the colonists—especially in the southern region—were afraid the Somerset case would be a threat to their growing agrarian economy.

While there were many factors that fueled the War of Independence, there's no denying that our young country's reliance on slavery was one of them. With a continued emphasis on the more progressive founding fathers like Ben Franklin and John Adams, our nation has a history of forgetting its dark past, which includes the barbaric executions of Mark and Phillis.

Sadly, America was built on the backs of slaves, and its land is stained with their blood.

LOUISA MAY ALCOTT

When the cast filmed the 2019 remake of Louisa May Alcott's classic *Little Women*, they stayed at Concord's Colonial Inn, and many of the actors felt like the ghost of the famous author had somehow followed them on set.

Alcott's semi-autobiographical story chronicles the lives of the four March sisters—Meg, Jo, Beth and Amy—and details their journey from adolescence into womanhood. Alcott wrote the coming-of-age novel in 1868, and the American author's childhood home, Orchard House, served as the inspiration for the homestead in *Little Women* and is now a museum in Concord. This historic house on Lexington Road is also believed to be the postmortem gathering spot for the Alcott family spirits.

"What's incredible about being in Concord is that you'll say in this shy way, 'I sort of feel the spirit of Louisa,' and locals will say, 'Oh yeah. That's haunted. We see her all the time. She walks with the girls all the time,'" said Laura Dern, who played Marmee March in the movie, in an interview with OprahMag.com.

The writer and director of the *Little Women* movie, Greta Gerwig, echoed Dern's sentiment and told the *Hollywood Reporter* that she was "seized by the spirit of Louisa May Alcott" and had a spiritual connection with the late author that inspired her to retell the story inspired by Alcott's childhood in Concord.

Beth van Duzer, the former general manager of a local ghost tour, told *Concord Journal* that Alcott was convinced that Orchard House was haunted by a family member. "Van Duzer said Louisa herself felt a presence in the house, that of her late sister, Lizzie, who inspired the character of Beth in

The Alcott Room at Concord's Colonial Inn pays homage to Louisa May Alcott, the author of *Little Women*. *Courtesy of Concord's Colonial Inn.*

the book," reported Christen Kelley in the September 28, 2021 edition of the *Wicked Local* newspaper. "Although Lizzie never lived at Orchard House, her spirit followed her sisters to their new home."

According to the tour guide and local historian, visitors have reported seeing faces in the windows of Orchard House and confirmed that many of the actors on set for the 2019 remake of *Little Women* strongly felt like Alcott was on set throughout the filming process.

But why would Alcott continue to stick around? "I think a lot of these people that were here really liked being here," van Duzer added.

Rachel Handler, a reporter for *New York* magazine, attempted to communicate with Alcott's ghost in a fun article published with the group's website, Vulture.com, on December 31, 2019. In the aptly titled piece called "An Attempted Conversation with Louisa May Alcott's Ghost," Handler spent a few nights at Concord's Colonial Inn, where she teamed up with a psychic-medium, Angelina Diana.

Before heading to Orchard House, the duo checked out room 24 at the inn, where the medium picked up on a female spirit who seemed to be more like a psychic imprint and less intelligent in nature. "Residual energy, which is left from the people that used to live here; spiritual, which would be a ghost or a loved one; and psychokinetic, which we create with our brain," the psychic told Handler.

The reporter reached out to the locals about the ghosts at Concord's Colonial Inn for validation. Marie, a shopkeeper on Main Street, confirmed with Handler that room 24 is paranormally active. "It's a good place to have a séance," Marie said. "They're good ghosts, just stuck in the in-between."

After reaching out to the spirits of the inn, the team headed to Orchard House, where they met up with the house museum's executive director, Jan Turnquist. As with many of the local historical properties, the executive director shied away from talking about the Orchard House's reported ghosts.

However, the psychic-medium did pick up on lingering energy in the Alcotts' former home. She then tried her best to tap into the spirit energy of the famous author of *Little Women*.

"Louisa is contacting us," the medium said to the reporter and Turnquist. "The residual energy is bouncing off the walls. She's coming through you, Jan. You can't just read people without somebody present that has a connection, and you have a strong connection to her."

The psychic-medium then received spirit communication from Alcott about the Orchard House's structural issues. She also picked up on the

The Orchard House located on Lexington Road in Concord is well known for being where Louisa May Alcott wrote and set *Little Women* in 1868. *Courtesy of the Boston Public Library, Print Department.*

sounds of a phantom piano. While Turnquist didn't acknowledge that visitors have heard ghostly music inside the Orchard House, she did confirm that the Alcott family loved to play the piano and it was likely always in the background when Alcott wrote her books at a small desk in the upstairs bedroom.

As they were touring the museum, the reporter noticed a flower had fallen between the living and dining rooms. Was it a sign from Alcott's ghost? "You have to pay attention when things aren't where they're supposed to be," the medium told Handler. "Maybe she's saying hello, via paranormal activity. Maybe it's psychokinetic energy. There's some energy causing things to happen in this room."

While the article tiptoes around the possibility of paranormal activity and completely avoids the various reports of ghostly sightings at the house museum, the heart of the story is that Alcott's residual energy still lingers at her childhood home and the spirited inspiration behind *Little Women*—the emotions emanating from the author's tightknit family—has psychically imprinted itself into the Orchard House's walls.

NATHANIEL HAWTHORNE

Nathaniel Hawthorne, author of the classics *The Scarlet Letter* and *The House of the Seven Gables*, rented out the Old Manse from 1842 to 1845 with his lovely wife, Sophia Peabody, thanks to the support of their family friend Ralph Waldo Emerson.

Struggling financially, Hawthorne was forced to move back to his hometown of Salem, Massachusetts, after a three-year stint in Concord, where he worked for a short time as a customs inspector at the port. It was during this period that he wrote his bestselling novel following the trials and tribulations of Hester Prynne. Locals didn't like Hawthorne's depiction of Salem in the novel's introduction, so he quickly packed his bags and fled with Sophia.

"If I escape town without being tarred and feathered," Hawthorne later wrote to a friend, "I shall consider it good luck." The author and his wife returned in 1852 to Concord, where they bought the property formerly occupied by Louisa May Alcott's family now called the Wayside. He's buried next to Sophia at Authors Ridge in Concord's Sleepy Hollow Cemetery. Hawthorne passed on May 19, 1864, at the age of fifty-nine.

While on a tour of the White Mountains, Nathaniel Hawthorne died in his sleep on May 19, 1864, in Plymouth, New Hampshire. He's buried at Authors Ridge in Concord's Sleepy Hollow Cemetery. *Courtesy of the Boston Public Library, Print Department.*

There's an obvious supernatural tone to his writing that seemed to be inspired by his experiences in Salem and Concord. Did Hawthorne, however, actually believe in ghosts? Based on the themes he explored in his books, the iconic author may have, but he definitely had a healthy dose of skepticism that seemed to change over time.

His friend William Baker Pike worked with Hawthorne at the Salem Custom House in the 1840s. Pike, a Swedenborgian spiritualist, strongly believed in the idea of communicating with the dead. However, the author initially had his doubts. "Hawthorne was a skeptic, but he treated Pike's belief with respect," wrote Margaret Moore in *The Salem World of Nathaniel Hawthorne.*

In fact, Hawthorne wrote about his skepticism in a letter to Pike dated July 24, 1851. "I should be very glad to believe that these rappers are, in any one instance, the spirits of the persons whom they profess themselves to be; but though I have talked with those who have had the freest communication, there has always been something that makes me doubt."

While Hawthorne was initially a skeptic, he started to explore the possibility of the existence of spirits in his fiction. His book *The House of the Seven Gables* hinted at the supernatural with one character, Alice Pyncheon, being driven mad by a spell and dying from shame. Her spirit haunts the gabled house. Also, the building's original owner, Matthew Maule, makes a postmortem return to his ancestral dwelling in the novel.

Hawthorne's skeptical tune changed later in his life. In a story written in hindsight and published posthumously, the author claimed that he had a close encounter with a haunting while hanging out at the Boston Athenaeum, a members-only research facility considered to be the nation's oldest library, founded in 1807. It was a private gentleman's club, hosting luminaries such as Henry Wadsworth Longfellow, Henry David Thoreau and, of course, Hawthorne, who read books and shared ideas.

Yes, it was a gentleman's club—no, not that kind of gentleman's club.

According to his published account called *The Ghost of Doctor Harris*, the famed writer in residence was eating breakfast one morning at the library's former Pearl Street location when he noticed a familiar face reading the *Boston Post*. It was Dr. Thaddeus Mason Harris, a well-known Unitarian clergyman from Dorchester, sitting in his usual chair in front of the library's second-floor fireplace. Hawthorne didn't bother the old patriarch. However, he was shocked to learn later that night that the Athenaeum regular had passed away.

Hawthorne returned to the Athenaeum the following day and noticed, completely in shock, Harris sitting at his usual spot and reading the newspaper. Yep, Hawthorne spotted the deceased doctor, looking "gaseous and vapory," and he was completely dumbfounded.

According to lore, Hawthorne spotted Harris's ghost for six weeks, and he later told his editor that he wished he had confronted the apparition. He wanted to ask him, "So, what's it like to be dead?" or at least find out if the old man knew he had passed. In fact, Hawthorne joked with his editor about the Harris encounter, saying, "Perhaps he finally got to his obituary and realized he was dead."

When the library moved to its current posh 10½ Beacon Street location across from the Massachusetts State House in 1847, Harris's ghost reportedly followed the Athenaeum's antiquarian books and his own nineteenth-century portrait. In fact, Harris's misty apparition has been spotted waiting to take the elevator to the structure's top floor.

"Most people believe this to be the ghost of the reverend that Hawthorne saw many years ago," remarked Christopher Forest in *Boston's Haunted History*. "The library was moved from that Pearl Street location to the present-day location near the Boston Common decades ago. However, it would appear that didn't stop the dear Reverend Harris from following the books and moving to the new library. Many people think Harris still rides an elevator to the third floor, so many years after he last visited the old building."

The Boston Athenaeum now opens its red door to the public in guided tours. However, the so-called haunted elevator is off-limits to visitors, wrote *Ghosts of Boston Town* author Holly Nadler.

"The public is barred from using the haunted elevator, which rises and falls of its own accord as if prankish spirits amuse themselves by flitting in and out of the cabin, pushing buttons for all five floors," Nadler mused. "According to Boston ghost hunter Jim McCabe, thousands of dollars have been poured into fixing the elevator's unending glitches, to no avail."

In 2002, the Athenaeum bought a brand-new elevator—and it's still acting up. Recent visitors who toured the library contend that the lift still has a mind of its own.

RALPH WALDO EMERSON

Where's Waldo? If you're looking for the ghost of Ralph Waldo Emerson, the famous transcendentalist poet and lecturer, pay a visit to his old Ivy League stomping ground in Cambridge, Massachusetts. While he was born in Boston on May 25, 1803, and buried at Concord's Sleepy Hollow Cemetery in 1882, he spent his formative years as a starving student studying at Harvard Divinity School in the "City of Squares."

One of Emerson's old haunts on campus was the university's historic Wadsworth House located at 1341 Massachusetts Avenue.

Built in 1726, this Early Georgian building is one of the few large houses not constructed by a Tory. Facing Massachusetts Avenue and an

Ralph Waldo Emerson died in Concord on April 27, 1882, and his grave is marked by a marble boulder on Authors Ridge in Sleepy Hollow Cemetery. *Courtesy of Concord's Colonial Inn.*

architectural anomaly of sorts thanks to its five-bay façade and simplistic Colonial design, Wadsworth House served as the primary residence for the president of Harvard until 1849. Over the years, the house would host visiting ministers and student boarders, including Emerson. The second-oldest surviving structure on Harvard's campus, the house lost its front yard when Massachusetts Avenue was widened.

Wadsworth House was also a major player in the days leading up to the Revolutionary War. The fight for independence began on April 19, 1775, and thousands of armed men from all over New England gathered in Cambridge. However, there was a housing shortage. Soldiers camped in the Cambridge Common while Harvard, responding to the growing anti-Tory sentiment and concerned about student safety, canceled classes on May 1 and allowed displaced soldiers to set up temporary shelter in its buildings. Oddly, classes took a wartime field trip nearly twenty miles away in Concord when classes resumed on October 5.

On June 15, 1775, the Continental Congress appointed George Washington as commander in chief of the army, and he assumed his role as the leader of the troops on July 3, 1775. Washington set up his first headquarters at Wadsworth House, located at 1341 Massachusetts Avenue, and it's said that he hashed out plans to oust King George from Boston in the historic landmark's parlor room. Washington, who remained in Cambridge until April 1776, later moved into his primary residence located at the Longfellow House on Brattle Street. Apparently, Wadsworth was in complete disrepair at the time.

In addition to its role in the Revolutionary War, there are several reports of Washington-era residual hauntings that continue to linger in the chambers of the colonial haunt. "One account explains that early one morning, forty years ago, a cleaning lady vacuuming alone in Wadsworth House saw a grim character in a tricorn hat and cloak silently come down the stairs and go out the door," reported the *Crimson* in 1997. The reporter, however, never confirmed the rumor, adding that "none of the staff at the Wadsworth House have heard anything about a man in a tricorn hat."

An article dating back to 1986 confirmed a similar story. "Over at Wadsworth House, where Washington once slept, ghosts of American Patriots wearing tricorn hats and cloaks have not haunted the colonial building in at least twenty-five years," the *Crimson* added.

Spirits wearing tricorn hats? Yep, Harvard Square allegedly has them. For the record, a residual haunting isn't technically a ghost but a playback or recording of a past event. Based on the so-called Stone Tape theory, these apparitions aren't intelligent spirits that interact with the living but psychic imprints that happen especially during moments of high tension, such as a murder or intense moments of a person's life. According to the hypothesis, residual hauntings are simply non-interactive playbacks, similar to a movie.

Based on ghost lore, hauntings have been associated with the lack of proper burial or a later desecration of the grave. Countless spirits, according to paranormal researchers, have been traced to missing gravestones or vandalism of a resting place. In regard to the pre-Revolution spirit allegedly lingering in Wadsworth House, it's likely that the residual haunting is a psychic imprint of sorts associated with the intense military strategy sessions in the summer of 1775.

In November 1973, the senior editor of *Harvard Magazine*, with offices formerly located in the Wadsworth House, wrote an article called "The House Is Haunted and We Like It That Way," referring to the tricorn hat–wearing spirits allegedly haunting the almost three-hundred-year-old landmark. "For a society of rationalists, Harvardians are surprisingly interested in the supernatural," mused *Harvard Magazine*'s editor in 1998. "Clearly, all this talk about ghosts concerns Harvard's continuity and history and traditions—not séances and the ectoplasm."

The Ralph Waldo Emerson house was built in 1828 and is a four-square, two-story frame structure located in Concord. *Courtesy of the Boston Public Library, Print Department.*

Seriously? Based on reports from the cleaning lady who spotted the "grim character in a tricorn hat and cloak" levitating down the stairs, perhaps the ghosts of Harvard are more than a personification of the Ivy League's storied past. It's possible that the spirits of Wadsworth House are, in fact, ghostly reminders of the historically significant military sessions spearheaded by Washington in 1775.

Of course, Emerson is synonymous with Concord. After spending time as a youth at the Old Manse, he purchased a property in Concord that his family affectionately called "Bush." Emerson, who penned his book-length essay "Nature" in 1836 and "Self Reliance" in 1841, composed most of his famous works while living in Concord.

On July 24, 1872, the roof and much of the second floor of his homestead were destroyed by fire. Locals rallied together and saved Emerson's books and manuscripts. They also chipped in to help Emerson repair the house that he and his family lived in for fifty years until his death in 1882.

If Emerson, who went by his middle name Waldo, is sticking around in the afterlife, he's likely hanging out at his old home, which is now a house museum in Concord. Or is he? As Emerson lamented during one of his lectures at Harvard, "The whole world is an omen and a sign. Why look so wistfully in a corner? Man is the image of God. Why run after a ghost or a dream?"

THE NEIGHBORS

My experience working at Concord's Colonial Inn reminded me of other historic locations in the area known for their Revolutionary War–era ghosts. Over the years, I've interviewed several innkeepers and property managers who strongly believed that ghosts scare customers away. Other locations have learned to embrace their hauntings.

The Colonial Inn has successfully showcased its "rooms with a boo" by redirecting paranormal enthusiasts to two of the suites in the main inn and hosting several events including "Dining with the Dead," organized by my good friends Tom D'Agostino and Arlene Nicholson.

Not everyone who manages historically haunted locations, however, knows how to walk the line.

For a few months during the summer of 2018, I served as a docent at the Shirley-Eustis House located in the Roxbury neighborhood of Boston, Massachusetts. And, yes, my short stint giving tours of historic property was spirited to say the least.

Built in 1747 by William Shirley, the royal governor of the Province of Massachusetts Bay, the property was later occupied by Colonel Asa Witcomb's Sixth Foot Regiment, and in 1778, it was seized and sold as a Loyalist property. The mansion sat vacant for several years until William Eustis, a congressman who also served as the secretary of war under James Madison's presidency during the War of 1812, acquired the house with his wife, Caroline Langdon Eustis.

The Shirley-Eustis House in Boston. *Photo by Frank C. Grace.*

As soon as I walked into the Georgian-style mansion nicknamed "Shirley Place" by its previous owners, I was contacted by the female spirit of the house, Madame Eustis. She whispered what sounded like my name in my ear. I then started to communicate with her using my L-shaped dowsing rods.

The matriarch of the Shirley-Eustis House let me know in no uncertain terms that she didn't like some of the furniture in the first-floor "drawing room" and also seemed desperate to find out what happened to a painting that was removed after she died in 1865. For the record, the mansion was divided into fifty-three units and sold two years after her death. Her artwork and a majority of her belongings were sold at auction in 1867.

The room where Eustis and his wife entertained visitors like the Marquis de Lafayette in 1824 and other luminaries like John Quincy Adams, Henry Clay, Daniel Webster and Aaron Burr did feature a replica of the famed portrait of William Eustis painted in 1804. The original by Gilbert Stuart is owned by the Met in Manhattan.

While working as a tour guide at the mansion, I encountered the ghost of Madame Eustis on a regular basis. She seemed to linger in the drawing room, solemnly looking out of the window facing what was her sanctuary, the estate's orchard and gardens. Based on the spirit's point of view, she could also see the historic carriage house, salvaged from Isabella Stewart Gardner's property in Brookline.

One Sunday afternoon, I decided to check out the off-limits attic of the mansion. There was a room known as the "Prophet's Chamber," which was used as a makeshift recovery room for bedridden victims of the Revolutionary War. As I was inspecting the weathered attic, I noticed what looked like original yellow wallpaper and signs of a fire indicated by the scorch marks in the historic wooden beams.

I also spotted a stain on the wall that clearly resembled a bloody handprint. Was it paint or something more sinister?

During the American Revolution, the Sixth Foot Regiment occupied the house. Meanwhile, Eustis was an up-and-coming surgeon. In fact, he served under Dr. Joseph Warren, who was fatally wounded at the Battle of Bunker Hill. Eustis was also a known "spunker," or a member of a secret group of Harvard medical students known to steal cadavers that were used for anatomy dissections in medical school.

While it's rumored that Eustis may have practiced medicine at the mansion, it's my guess that the bloody handprint was left from one of the soldiers recovering in the "Prophet's Chamber" during the War for Independence.

The Shirley-Eustis House had many secrets. And based on my interactions with Madame Eustis, I knew that the spirits of the mansion had the answers.

When I was approached by the lead docent to come up with ideas to generate much-needed revenue to help with the preservation efforts of the mansion, I suggested candlelight ghost tours or paranormal investigations. She loved the idea and pitched it to the interim executive director. The response, however, was less than favorable. I was pulled into a closed-door meeting by one of the members from the Board of Governors. The volunteer mocked the idea, sarcastically saying that she "talked with the ghosts of the house and they asked to be left alone." She also said that the board wouldn't approve the ghost tours, which were to be led by battery-operated lanterns, because of the additional electricity costs.

After the uncomfortable meeting, the lead docent was let go, and I quickly resigned from a position that I genuinely loved. The experience left me with even more unanswered questions. It didn't make sense to me. Why?

Michelle Hamilton, manager of the Mary Washington House in Fredericksburg, Virginia, and author of *Civil War Ghosts*, told me that the answer is as diverse as each historical site. "One reason is that the paranormal is a belief system; either you believe in ghosts or you don't," she said. Hamilton added that religious beliefs play a huge part in the decision to open the doors to investigative teams. "Many view ghost tours and investigations as being disrespectful of the dead," she explained, "that ghost tours make money from the suffering of the dead."

Hamilton said that the myths and misconceptions perpetuated by ill-informed guides generally don't help the cause. "A focus on diligent historic research in the field beyond just capturing another EVP saying 'get out!' will help improve the reputation of paranormal investigators," she said. "Another concern expressed by historical organizations is that the museum or property will become only known for its ghosts. The fear is that the site will become akin to a fun house attraction," Hamilton told me. "Also there's a risk of damage or vandalism to an historic site by investigators or the public."

Point made. In recent years, however, there seems to have been a noticeable shift among heritage organizations becoming more open-minded to spirits while embracing the haunted history of the properties that they oversee. Of course, not all heritage groups are so forthcoming when it comes to the paranormal.

Tim Weisberg, host of the *Midnight in the Desert* podcast and author of *Ghosts of the SouthCoast*, told me that he's encountered a few roadblocks over the years from the overseers of historic locations with ghostly backstories.

"For a region that is so integral to the history of our country, it seems as though the paranormal is not an acceptable topic for a majority of historic sites and heritage organizations," Weisberg said. "One of the main reasons for that, I believe, is that there is an 'old guard' that oversees many of these locations. They're people that got involved in preserving history decades ago, and they see paranormal research as an affront to what it is they've been doing all of these years. It's considered tacky and gives off the wrong impression, they'll tell you."

Weisberg believes that New England's closed-minded Puritan ethos may be responsible for the "no ghost" mentality. "In actuality, the paranormal is how these sites will find the next generation of stewards," he said. "Young people are more interested in the haunts than the history, and someone needs to be ready to take over these sites or they'll fall by the wayside. Why not embrace the ghosts if it means someone will ensure the location lives on?"

When asked why some groups embrace the paranormal while others are less enthusiastic, Weisberg believes that money is a huge factor. "Those who understand that allowing paranormal investigation of their historic sites could lead to new fundraising avenues are usually the ones that are most willing to let us in," he said. "The other factor is if the docents and employees are having their own paranormal experiences and they actually think the place is haunted, they're more apt to allow us in so that we can help them further explore what's been happening to them."

There has also been a shift with paranormal-themed shows, like *Kindred Spirits* and programs that he's worked on, including *Haunted Towns*, to research and accurately portray the backstories of the historic locations on television. Weisberg's motto at the events he has hosted has been "come for the haunts, stay for the history," which echoes the trend to spotlight historical accuracy.

"The key is to show these organizations that as much as we're looking to capture data on investigations that may or may not prove the existence of ghosts, it's still one of our primary goals to accurately share and understand the history of these locations," Weisberg said. "Who better to tell that story than the spirits of those who lived through it?"

Monument Square

As one of the first inland settlements established by the English in 1635, Concord became a hotspot for colonial unrest. The First Massachusetts Provincial Congress gathered there in 1774 where the First Parish Church Meeting House is located today. The John Hancock–led Second Congress also met in Monument Square in 1775.

Soon after the rabble-rouser Patriots secretly gathered in town, the British marched into Concord determined to destroy a gunpowder cache and arrest Hancock and Samuel Adams in the process.

Guests visiting Concord's town center report the sounds of horses galloping up and down Monument Street. In addition to the disembodied echoes of hooves clopping on cobblestones and what sounds like a large animal snorting, there are several eyewitness accounts of a colonial-era man on horseback that appears to be a residual haunting or a videotape-like replay of an event that occurred years ago. The glowing apparition looks like he's searching for something near the Wright Tavern.

Why would a minuteman from the 1700s leave a psychic imprint that eerily includes his equine friend? Gare Allen, a Florida-based author armed with more than a dozen paranormal-themed books, is my usual go-to expert when it comes to animal spirits. During the research phase of this book, I noticed a recurring theme with the paranormal activity that I encountered specifically near the battlefield: phantom *Equus caballus*.

Yes, ghost horses. I trotted over to Allen for advice.

"It doesn't surprise me when someone shares their encounter with the spirit of an animal, especially those that we formed a bond with during

Monument Square is across the street from Concord's Colonial Inn and is named for its Civil War memorial obelisk erected in 1866. *Courtesy of the Boston Public Library, Print Department.*

their corporeal lives," Allen said. "Pets are often considered members of the family, and their loss can be just as devastating as that of a human loved one."

Galloping ghosts? Allen told me that the phenomenon is usually tied to their two-legged counterparts.

"The soldier-horse relationship during wartime must have been complex given the dangerous conditions," he explained. "Their mutual safety was quite dependent on each other's cooperation and inherent will to survive. The soldier's commitment to the horse's needs of food, water and treatment of injuries undoubtedly fostered trust and loyalty. Similarly, a soldier's life literally rested on the strength of his stallion's back."

Allen believes that the soldiers and horses developed a bond while navigating the life-and-death dangers of the Revolutionary War. "Action and instinct had to become one, as did the desire to survive," he said. "As with human ghosts, perhaps the sightings of horse spirits on the battlefields of our past can be explained in the same fashion. Some searching for their former riders, some trapped between worlds, and others could be a harsh imprint of suffering so haunting that it stamped itself in time."

This sort of psychic imprint or residual haunting has also been reported at the Old South Meeting House in Boston. Giddyup?

There's an eerie silence when one opens the hallowed white doors and walks into this important Revolutionary War–era structure. Inside, visitors can see where Ben Franklin was baptized and, more importantly, where Samuel Adams fueled the whole "no taxation without representation" Patriot war cry against British rule.

The Boston Tea Party rally was originally slated for Faneuil Hall, but it was moved to the Old South Meeting House because it was large enough to handle the spillover masses. At the time, it was the largest building in colonial Boston. Old South was also where thousands of outraged Bostonians gathered to protest the Boston Massacre in March 1770, in which five colonists were killed by British soldiers.

Built in 1729 by a Puritan congregation who probably had no idea that this Freedom Trail favorite would play such an important role in American history as the go-to gathering place of record for more than three centuries, the Old South Meeting House is also reportedly haunted.

Michael Baker, a former investigator with Para-Boston, organized a paranormal investigation at the historic building. Their findings? The paranormal investigation team did record an EVP (electromagnetic voice phenomenon) of a male voice saying, "Who's there?" There were also firsthand accounts of chains rattling in the lower area of the OSMH and a bizarre recording anomaly coming from the building's steeple.

Was any evidence discovered of a Revolutionary War–era horse spirit lingering in the building, as some have suggested? Nay…or should that be *neighhhh*? Unless the EVP was of a dead Mr. Ed. However, several visitors to the building have reported smelling hay, and one woman who tied the knot in the Old South Meeting House said she had a close encounter with the horse spirit.

For the record, the redcoats ransacked the building during the Revolutionary War and used it as a horse stable and riding school for British soldiers. George Washington walked by the building during the late 1700s and was extremely unhappy with how the Brits had desecrated this important landmark.

Similar to Boston's Old South Meeting House, Concord's Wright Tavern played an equally significant role during the 1700s. And much like its counterpart, the historic watering hole, which was built in 1747 by Ephraim Jones, is also believed to be haunted by the ghosts of its Revolutionary War past.

"No historic building in Concord is more important to the American Revolution than the Wright Tavern," reported Melvin H. Bernstein in *Wicked Local*. "Yet the story of the Wright Tavern is little told, under-appreciated, and largely taken for granted."

The new Provincial Congress of Massachusetts held committee meetings there on October 11, 1774, where they hammered out resolutions regarding military, safety and tax collections in preparation for what became the

American Revolution. Also, in the wee hours of April 19, 1775, the militia gathered at the tavern kept by Amos Wright as they prepared for the looming confrontation at Old North Bridge.

After the war, the tavern became a bakery before it was sold in 1831. After hosting a revolving door of tenants that included a print shop, the structure was purchased by Reuben Rice and former U.S. attorney general Ebenezer Hoar and was converted back to its original use as an inn. It was formerly used by the Concord Museum for educational programming and is currently occupied by an architectural firm.

People who have visited the historic structure have reported feeling an inexplicable energy when they walked into the historic tavern and what sounded like disembodied voices coming from rooms that were unoccupied. Of course, there's the phantom colonist on horseback spotted right outside the tavern in Monument Square.

Is Concord's Wright Tavern haunted? Possibly, but it appears to be residual in nature.

Historically, these colonial-era watering holes served as "nerve centers for spreading vital news and sanctuaries for outlawed organizations," wrote Roxie Zwicker in *Haunted Pubs of New England*. "Certain pubs bore witness to ghastly deeds and sorrowful tragedies. Some of them became tinged with the aura of the supernatural."

Perhaps the ghostly man seen on horseback outside Wright Tavern is stopping by for some spirited conversation and to down an ale or two in the afterlife.

Whoa, Nellie.

Sleepy Hollow Cemetery

Authors Ridge in Concord's Sleepy Hollow Cemetery is the final resting spot for some of New England's more celebrated writers, including Henry David Thoreau, Louisa May Alcott, Nathaniel Hawthorne and Ralph Waldo Emerson. Designed in the early nineteenth century, the graveyard was intentionally created as a "garden of the living" to encourage visitors to enjoy the picturesque scenery while honoring the departed.

For the record, the cemetery in Concord is often confused with the old cemetery in Tarrytown, New York, made famous by Washington Irving's "The Legend of Sleepy Hollow" short story. Sorry, but there's no headless horseman in this serene final resting place for Concord's literary elite.

There is one alleged haunting, however, at Concord's Sleepy Hollow Cemetery involving the eerie grave of Ephraim Bull. He wasn't a writer—or a decapitated Hessian soldier—but the visionary was the first to cultivate the Concord grape. Apparently, Bull was a bitter man when he died because he never saw any profits from the fruits of his lifelong work. His tomb is inscribed, "He sowed, others reaped."

If it's true that there's postmortem unrest associated with unfinished business, Bull's spirit probably does linger among the skeletal remains of America's elite nineteenth-century writers in Concord.

Oddly, there's only one ghost story associated with Sleepy Hollow Cemetery. Why? It's a common belief that the paranormal activity at New England's haunted cemeteries is psychic remnants of the unjust killings and unmarked graves leftover from centuries of tainted dirt from the region's dark past.

There's an inexplicable feeling of tranquility when entering Sleepy Hollow—with no signs of disrespect or desecrated graves. Of course, not all cemeteries are doom and gloom. People say "rest in peace" when a loved one passes for a reason, and that's certainly the case with Sleepy Hollow Cemetery.

Brian Gerraughty, a paranormal investigator with the Greater Boston Paranormal Associates and a frequent visitor to notoriously haunted cemeteries, told me that it makes sense that burial grounds are more paranormally active compared to other locations he's investigated. "It has been my personal experience and also from discussions with others in the field that many spirits visit their resting places occasionally to connect with those left behind," Gerraughty said. "It would be a logical place for two planes of existence to overlap."

However, not all paranormal investigators believe cemeteries are haunted hotspots. In fact, Tina Storer, formerly from the TV show *Ghost Bait*, told me most of the supposedly haunted graveyards she visited during her paranormal investigation days were overrated. "It's easy to think of cemeteries as being haunted. It's a place associated with death. But I don't think it's any different than any other location personally," Storer said. "Spirits are everywhere, and cemeteries are just pinpointing a location to their place of rest."

Michael Baker, a scientific-minded paranormal investigator formerly with Para-Boston, echoed Storer's belief. The researcher conducted an exhaustive study for his New England Center for the Advancement of Paranormal Science (NECAPS) on points of geothermal and electromagnetic energy in New England in an attempt to predict active locations. According to Baker, patterns did emerge, including a preponderance of paranormal incidents along fault lines, railroad tracks and areas where there are higher reports of UFO sightings. However, the study concluded that graveyards were oddly void of activity. "We left no stone unturned, even cemeteries," Baker said. "We found that there is no correlation to hauntings and cemeteries, which goes against what a lot of people believe."

Sleepy Hollow Cemetery is a picturesque rural cemetery located on Bedford Street near the center of Concord. *Courtesy of the Boston Public Library, Print Department.*

If Sleepy Hollow Cemetery isn't haunted, then maybe visitors could learn from their turn-of-the-century predecessors and just chill with Concord's literary elite. In addition to paying respect to the dead, burial grounds also served as park and recreation areas during the late nineteenth century. In fact, it was common during the Victorian era for Americans to picnic in graveyards.

Yes, people would actually "dig in" at cemeteries—and we're not talking about grave diggers.

"It wasn't just apple-munching alongside the winding avenues of graveyards," wrote Jonathan Kendall in *Atlas Obscura.* "Since many municipalities still lacked proper recreational areas, many people had full-blown picnics in their local cemeteries. The tombstone-laden fields were the closest things, then, to modern-day public parks."

Not hungry? Psychic-medium Kristen Cappucci jokingly told me that cemeteries are almost like postmortem party spots for spirits. Wanna dance with the dead? Then head to Concord's Sleepy Hollow Cemetery and waltz with legends like Alcott, Hawthorne and Thoreau.

If dining—or dancing—with the dead isn't your thing, an idea is to learn the basics of paranormal investigating at a not-so-haunted graveyard like Sleepy Hollow Cemetery. Demonologist James Annitto told me that it's perfect for beginners looking to learn the tricks of the trade.

Annitto said historic burial grounds like the well-known one in Concord may have "lots of contamination, but that's what makes you a great investigator and how you learn," adding that outdoor locations are difficult for the most experienced paranormal investigators because of false-positive readings on equipment because of noise, temperature fluctuations and wind. "It gives you the ability to decipher what's contamination and what is plausible paranormal activity. I started out doing graveyards and cemeteries. You would just need to call and get permission."

THE OLD MANSE

If you ask locals to point out the most haunted locations in Concord, the Old Manse near North Bridge is often mentioned along with its notoriously haunted neighbor, the Colonial Inn. Built in 1770 by the Reverend William Emerson, the Georgian clapboard house overlooks the Concord River and had a bird's-eye view of one of the most pivotal moments in the nation's early history, the Battles of Lexington and Concord and the "shot heard 'round the world" on April 19, 1775. From the second-floor window of the Old Manse, the Reverend Emerson watched in horror as both British and Patriot soldiers started to fire their weapons. He also witnessed the controversial killing of two British soldiers by the hatchet-wielding Ammi White.

Yes, the land surrounding the Old Manse is stained with blood.

In the 1800s, some of New England's most revered authors were inspired by the Old Manse. Ralph Waldo Emerson and Nathaniel Hawthorne both lived in the historic home. Emerson drafted his influential essay "Nature" in an upstairs study. Hawthorne and his wife, Sophia, started their married life there in 1842, and *Walden* author Henry David Thoreau re-created an heirloom vegetable garden as a wedding gift for the newly married Hawthornes.

During their residence in the Old Manse, Nathaniel and Sophia had their first child, Una, who was born on March 3, 1844. In 1845, the Hawthornes left Concord for Salem after struggling to pay the rent. In honor of his short but memorable stay, Hawthorne penned a collection of stories called *Mosses from an Old Manse* in 1846.

"Nathanial Hawthorne believed he would hear Ezra Ripley, the preacher who lived in the house before him," reported tour guide and local historian Beth van Duzer in the September 28, 2021 edition of the *Concord Journal*. "He said he would feel him walk by and feel his silk robes go by him," she said.

In the days leading up to Halloween, tour guides open up the Old Manse's attic, where the servants are said to still haunt the property. Hawthorne and his wife, Sophia, would report hearing noises from the attic in the wee hours

In 1842, Nathaniel Hawthorne rented the Old Manse in Concord, Massachusetts, for $100 a year. He moved in with his wife, transcendentalist Sophia Peabody, on July 9, 1842, as newlyweds. *Photo by Jason Baker.*

of the night. "She would grind coffee and they'd hear her ironing, but every morning they'd wake up and there's nothing to show for this servant's work," van Duzer told the *Concord Journal*. "I'd like to go on the record and say, if ghosts want to make me coffee, I'm OK with it."

According to the article, docents at the Old Manse report lights turning on and off without explanation and objects moving from one floor to another by its ghostly caretakers.

While the Old Manse hasn't opened its doors to paranormal investigators for many years, veteran investigator Don DeCristofaro remembers connecting with Hawthorne's spirit at the house. "When we were at the Old Manse, we were in Nathaniel Hawthorne's writing room, and we strongly started to smell cigar smoke. That was the first time during an investigation that we picked up olfactory evidence," DeCristofaro told me. "We also had a table-tipping session. We asked a number of questions that really pinned down the fact that we were talking to Nathaniel Hawthorne himself."

DeCristofaro said the investigation at the Old Manse was early in his ghost-hunting career and ultimately inspired him to form his group called the Greater Boston Paranormal Associates. "We asked him if he had a shoulder injury and he said 'yes,' and we asked if he fell off a horse," he said. "We also asked him if he was a writer, and all questions validated that it was, in fact, Nathaniel Hawthorne."

There have been reports from tour guides and visitors that the Old Manse is also haunted by a female energy. Some believe it's the ghost of the first lady of the house, Phebe Bliss Emerson Ripley. "She was the wife of the Reverend William Emerson and Dr. Ripley," said James St. Vincent, a former tour guide in Concord. "She had a huge hand in the design of the house. It was her home. I can't imagine she would think otherwise even in death."

The female spirit of the house has been seen standing in front of the window on the second floor and eerily watching people as they approach the property. Tour guides are often asked about a woman wearing period garb, and the guests are shocked to find out that no one in the house museum is dressed in costume.

While many believe the lady in white is Phebe, others have suggested that the phantom in the window is a psychic imprint left by Hawthorne's wife, Sophia, or possibly the disembodied spirit of a woman who tragically passed away outside the Old Manse in the Concord River.

On the first anniversary of Hawthorne's marriage, the *House of the Seven Gables* author and poet William Ellery Channing searched for a local woman who mysteriously disappeared. Martha Hunt's decomposing corpse was later found by Hawthorne and Channing in July 1843. She apparently drowned in the river behind the Old Manse.

"I never saw or imagined a spectacle of such perfect horror," Hawthorne wrote about the incident. "She was the very image of death-agony." Hawthorne's search for Martha inspired the climactic scene in his 1852 novel, *The Blithedale Romance*.

Others believe the spirit looking out the window at the Old Manse is Hawthorne's wife, Sophia. While the couple struggled financially to pay the $100-a-year rent, the newlyweds seemed to be happy in Concord and etched affectionate notes into the windowpanes in the upstairs room that Hawthorne used as a study. "Man's accidents are God's purposes," wrote Sophia Peabody Hawthorne in 1843.

Hawthorne initially met Sophia at a lavish dinner party at the Peabody family home located at 53 Charter Street in Hawthorne's hometown, literally next door to the Old Burying Point in Salem. The house next to the cemetery served as inspiration for Hawthorne's *Dr. Grimshawe's Secret*.

According to lore, Sophia suffered from migraines, and the couple would take midnight strolls in the cemetery. It's believed that the headaches were the result of drugs her father, a Salem dentist, prescribed to her during early childhood to ease her difficulty with teething.

Buried in Salem's Charter Street Cemetery is Hawthorne's ancestor John Hathorne, a witch-trials judge whose memory haunted him. According to local tours in the Witch City, Hawthorne added the *w* to his name to distance himself from his infamous great-great-grandfather. Yes, the writer allegedly abhorred his familial connection to the 1692 witch-trial hysteria. However, we can't prove historically that he added the *w* to his name because of the disdain.

At least eight members of his family were interred there, including his grandparents and two of their daughters. Witch-trial judge Bartholomew Gedney, poet Anne Bradstreet, architect-carver Samuel McIntire and *Mayflower* passenger Richard More are all buried there. No surprise, but names from the gravestones in the Charter Street Cemetery often appear in Hawthorne's writings. For example, the small gravestone of Hepzibah Packer, who died in 1885, possibly inspired Hawthorne to use the unusual name of Hepzibah in his novel *The House of the Seven Gables*. The same novel also features a character called "John Swinnerton," who shares his name with a real-life Salem doctor buried in the cemetery in the late seventeenth century.

While the Hawthornes are synonymous with Salem, the husband and wife are buried in Concord's Sleepy Hollow Cemetery, and it's said the two longed for the simpler times that they shared together as newlyweds at the Old Manse.

Perhaps the woman in white standing in front of the second-floor window of the historic home in Concord is indeed Hawthorne's wife Sophia gazing at the love notes she and her soon-to-be-famous husband etched into the windowpane more than a century ago.

CONCLUSION

During my six-month stint working the overnight shift at Concord's Colonial Inn, I was able to meet a motley crew of celebrities like Sarah Jessica Parker, who stayed at the inn while filming scenes for *Hocus Pocus 2* in Rhode Island.

And then there was the cast and crew for the horror-comedy flick called *The Parenting*, which centers on a young gay couple—played by Nik Dodani from *Atypical* and Brandon Flynn from *13 Reasons Why*—who host their inaugural parental meeting at a house inhabited by a four-hundred-year-old entity.

The producers for the HBO Max film wanted the cast to spend time at an actual haunted location, so they opted for Concord's Colonial Inn. The cast, which included Parker Posey, Brian Cox, Lisa Kudrow and Edie Falco, stayed in the cottage out back and the house across the street from the inn while the main couple, Dodani and Flynn, shacked up in two separate suites inside the main inn for weeks. Other players from the film, including Vivian Bang—known for her work in indie films like *White Rabbit*—and Dean Norris from *Breaking Bad*, also stayed indoors to get the full "haunted inn" experience.

The cast kept an open mind during their stay, hoping for a close encounter with one of the inn's resident spirits. Several of the film crew members talked about feeling an inexplicable energy, as if they stepped back in time, during their stay.

One of the actors, who asked to remain anonymous, confided to me that they kept waking up at 3:00 a.m. and would see strange light anomalies in their room. The actor tried to debunk it, believing the bizarre lights were

Nestled in a quaint New England village famed for its Revolutionary War and literary roots, Concord's Colonial Inn has hosted celebrities including John Wayne, Shirley Temple and the cast from the *Little Women* film remake in 2019. *Courtesy of Concord's Colonial Inn.*

from cars passing by from Lowell Road, but the suite was so high up from the ground floor it didn't make any sense. "The weirdest thing is that the lights were purple," the actor told me. "Does that mean anything?"

In the paranormal world, there's what we call the "purple light ray" from Archangel Zadkiel. The color signifies mercy and transformation.

I told the actor that I believe their sensitivities were being heightened while working on a paranormal-themed movie. "It sounds like you are tapping into something," I said. "It's like you're going through an awakening of sorts or you're really getting into character for your role."

A few days before the movie wrapped, I met up with Dodani, who initially claimed to be a skeptic but was interested when I told him I identified as a clairvoyant in addition to being an author of paranormal-themed books.

"You actually see dead people?" he asked. I sheepishly nodded and told him about the female spirit I spotted in his room in the past, which is the inn's Thoreau Suite situated right above the front desk area. "The woman seems to be a very nurturing spirit, as if she's a caregiver in the afterlife."

Psychics have called this female spirit "Rosemary" and believe she may have been a nurse during the American Revolution and possibly worked alongside Dr. Timothy Minot. As with several of the legends associated with Concord's Colonial Inn, however, there's no historical proof to validate Rosemary's existence.

Dodani did say that when he slept on the couch, which is where the spirit seemed to be sitting when I visited the room, he would sleep like a rock and would wake up completely refreshed. I mentioned to the actor that I would love to host a séance for a few of the cast members before they left the inn.

He agreed and invited two of my favorite actors from the movie, Parker Posey and Brandon Flynn. It turned out to be one of my most memorable séance experiences ever and included some messages from the other side as my friend Dana Masson, a high priestess witch, helped me lift the veil between the living and the dead.

Masson, who was my onscreen partner in the Salem documentary *Forbidden History*, picked up on two female spirits in the room. One was the nurturing energy that moves throughout the inn, while the second one didn't seem familiar to me at all.

I looked up. And I saw her.

As a clairvoyant, I sometimes get mind pictures, but in this situation, I clearly saw a woman appear in the corner of the room. She was wearing what looked like a blue house dress from the 1950s. As far as facial features, she actually looked a bit like Parker Posey, who was sitting to my right. The ghostly woman had high cheekbones and coiffed black hair and was holding her neck as if she was desperately trying to speak, but she couldn't.

She was panicking. Something was wrong.

Spirits have been spotted lounging in the chairs and lurking in the shadows of Concord's Colonial Inn by guests and employees. *Courtesy of Concord's Colonial Inn.*

I took a deep breath and proceeded with the séance for my actor friends. Lifting the veil that night was an amazing experience, but the traumatized female spirit standing in the corner continued to haunt me.

Who was she, and what did she want from me?

I reached out to my friends in the paranormal community to help me solve the mystery of the distraught lady I spotted during the séance with the cast of *The Parenting*. My friend and fellow author Joni Mayhan talked about a woman her group of empaths encountered during their baseline sweep at Concord's Colonial Inn years ago.

"As we investigated, we discovered a young woman in a hallway who hailed from the 1960s time period," Mayhan told me. "She was distraught and emotional and wasn't interested in talking with us."

When I reached out to Mayhan after my encounter with the disembodied soul during the séance, she strongly felt like we were talking about the same woman. "Yes, that certainly does sound like her," she confirmed. "I'm getting chills, so you're definitely on to something."

My friend and fellow clairvoyant Jeremy Cotter stopped by one morning while I was wrapping up my overnight shift a few days after the séance. He wanted to check in on me and see if he could help me give a voice to the ghost. When he arrived around 5:00 a.m., he told me that he had a spirit connection dream preparing him for his impromptu visit.

"I was connecting with a dark-haired woman. She's in her thirties. Not very tall. I would say just over five feet tall," he said. "She was very distraught and kept grasping at her neck in the vision."

Cotter continued, "She was standing near an old writing desk. This spirit dream happened recently when I was sleeping, and the nightmare woke me up at 3:00 a.m."

When I asked Cotter if the woman had ties to the inn, he shook his head. "No, I don't think she died here," he said. "I feel like her spirit was somehow drawn here. The inn is like a lighthouse to the spirit world. It's like a transient ghost hotel. You're going to get spirits that walk in and out like this dark-haired woman did after she died tragically. I'm getting that there was blunt force trauma to the head. She is looking for someone to help her."

Cotter's comments reminded me of an experience that a guest had many years ago while sleeping in room 24. The accounts are kept in a file logged by the inn's former front desk manager, Zachary Trznadel.

"Awakened by a flash of light early in the morning which didn't seem quite right, he soon went back to sleep. When he did he reported an incredibly vivid dream of a woman who sat in a wooden chair in the room, which was now transformed into how it must have looked a couple of decades ago. She spoke to him and said that she was the mistress of a man who lived here in Concord, who was now gone, and that they had used this room for their rendezvous," the front desk employee wrote in the staff log.

"The guest reported that the scene then changed and he saw the woman lying in her night clothes in bed, and a man entered the room, who then placed a pillow over her face and struck her with some sort of weapon," the guest continued.

The freaked-out visitor told the front desk staff that the dream ended with the voice of the female spirit saying, "My body was removed by others and taken away from here."

Was this the same woman?

Armed with the clues from my psychic-medium friends in the paranormal community plus my firsthand experience seeing her in the corner of the room during the séance, I started to do some preliminary research about the dark-haired lady haunting Concord's Colonial Inn.

While I couldn't find a cold case in the immediate area, there was a woman who mysteriously went missing in 1961 in nearby Lincoln, Massachusetts. The seemingly happy mother uncharacteristically disappeared and was spotted walking toward Concord sixty years ago and never heard from again.

When I saw her picture, I immediately thought to myself that she looks a lot like the spirit we've all seen at the inn. Out of respect for her family, I will refer to the woman as "Jane."

On October 24, 1961, police went to Jane's home in Lincoln after a neighbor reported seeing blood leading from the house to the driveway. She had made the discovery after a young girl returned from a friend's house to find her mother was nowhere to be found. In addition to the blood evidence, there were several unconfirmed sightings of a woman who appeared to be disoriented walking on nearby roads later that day.

Blood matching the missing woman's blood type was found in the kitchen, which indicated a likely abduction, although her two-year-old son was found safe asleep in his room. The plot thickened when a local reporter uncovered that the victim had borrowed several library books about murders and disappearances, including one that was eerily similar to her case

Local newspapers speculated that Jane had staged her disappearance while her husband was away on business in New York City, perhaps to escape issues at home. After investigating the missing woman's past, there was evidence of trauma associated with her childhood, which could have inspired her "gone girl" escape plan.

In addition to possibly staging her own disappearance, there were theories that she may have accidentally hit her head in the kitchen and suffered from amnesia or fallen at a construction site near the freeway. Or, as the police initially suspected during their initial investigation of her home in Lincoln in October 1961, she could have been abducted.

Jane's mysterious disappearance remains unsolved.

While I have no proof that the spirit I encountered during the séance was, in fact, Jane, I do believe that the Colonial serves as a "dead inn" for ghosts looking for postmortem closure. As my friend and fellow author Joni Mayhan told me, haunted hotels like Concord's Colonial Inn are far more paranormally active than most people would imagine. "If you consider the sheer number of people who stay in them, it makes perfect sense," Mayhan told me. "A normal house might encounter forty or fifty guests during the history of its existence, while a hotel will shelter that number in several days."

Before leaving my job as the night auditor at Concord's Colonial Inn, I said a prayer out loud for the spirits that I encountered along the way and thanked them for graciously welcoming me into their home. As I walked down the creaky wooden staircase one last time to clock out for my final graveyard shift in early July 2022, I promised to do my best to give them all a voice and tell their stories correctly.

Leaving Concord's Colonial Inn was like saying goodbye to an old friend. I took a deep breath and exhaled. Until next time.

SOURCES

U pdated excerpts from my first fourteen books, including *Ghosts of the American Revolution*, *Ghosts of Cambridge*, *Ghost Writers* and *Ghosts of Boston*, were featured in *Ghosts of Concord's Colonial Inn*.

The material in this book is drawn from published sources, including my articles in *DigBoston* and issues of *Boston Globe*, *Boston Herald*, *Boston Post*, *Concord Journal*, *Discover Concord*, *Harvard Crimson*, *Harvard Magazine*, *Herald News*, *Hollywood Reporter*, the *New York Times*, *Smithsonian* magazine and television programs like Travel Channel's *A Haunting*, *Psychic Kids* and classic episodes of *Ghost Hunters* currently streaming on Discovery+.

Several books on New England's paranormal history were used and cited throughout the text. Other websites and periodicals, like Peter Muise's New England Folklore, History.com, OprahMag.com, Vulture.com and Charles M. Skinner's *Myths & Legends of Our Own Land*, as well as the websites for Concord's Colonial Inn, Wicked Local and the National Park Service, also served as sources.

Most of the experts featured in this book, including Joni Mayhan, Richard Estep, Brian Cano, Gare Allen, Michelle Hamilton, Peter Muise and Tim Weisberg, are also authors, and I highly recommend their works as supplemental reading.

For the majority of *Ghosts of Concord's Colonial Inn*, I conducted firsthand interviews, and some of the material is drawn from my own research and information kept in a document by the inn's former manager Zachary Trznadel. Discussions with employees and guests at Concord's Colonial Inn served as major sources and generated original content. It should be noted that ghost stories are subjective, and I have made a concerted effort to stick to the historical facts, even if it resulted in debunking a legend that has been presented as fact over time.

Baltrusis, Sam. *Ghosts of Boston: Haunts of the Hub*. Charleston, SC: The History Press, 2012.

———. *Ghosts of Salem: Haunts of the Witch City*. Charleston, SC: The History Press, 2014.

———. *Ghosts of the American Revolution*. Guilford, CT: Globe Pequot Press, 2021.

———. *Ghost Writers: The Hallowed Haunts of Unforgettable Literary Icons*. Guilford, CT: Globe Pequot Press, 2019.

———. *Haunted Boston Harbor*. Charleston, SC: The History Press, 2016.

———. *13 Most Haunted Crime Scenes Beyond Boston*. Boston: Sam Baltrusis, 2016.

Beck, Derek W. *Igniting the American Revolution 1773–1775*. Naperville, IL: Sourcebooks, 2015.

D'Agostino, Thomas. *A Guide to Haunted New England*. Charleston, SC: The History Press, 2009.

Dudley, Dorothy. *Theatrum Majorum: The Cambridge of 1776*. Whitefish, MT: Kessinger Publishing, 2007.

French, Allen. *The First Year of the American Revolution*. Boston: Houghton Mifflin, 1934.

Hall, Thomas. *Shipwrecks of Massachusetts Bay*. Charleston, SC: The History Press, 2012.

Hauk, Dennis William. *Haunted Places: The National Directory*. New York: Penguin Group, 1996.

Mayhan, Joni. *Dark and Scary Things*. Gardner, MA: Joni Mayhan, 2015.

Muise, Peter. *Legends and Lore of the North Shore*. Charleston, SC: The History Press, 2014.

Nadler, Holly Mascott. *Ghosts of Boston Town: Three Centuries of True Hauntings*. Camden, ME: Down East Books, 2002.

Philbrick, Nathaniel. *Bunker Hill: A City, a Siege, a Revolution*. New York: Penguin Books, 2014.

Rapaport, Diane. *The Naked Quaker: True Crimes and Controversies*. Beverly, MA: Commonwealth Editions, 2007.

Revai, Cheri. *Haunted Massachusetts: Ghosts and Strange Phenomena of the Bay State*. Mechanicsburg, PA: Stackpole Books, 2005.

Rule, Leslie. *When the Ghost Screams: True Stories of Victims Who Haunt*. Kansas City, MO, n.d.

Stansfield, Charles A. *Haunted Presidents*. Mechanicsburg, PA: Stackpole Books, 2010.

Stark, James H. *The Loyalists of Massachusetts and the Other Side of the American Revolution*, Salem, MA: Salem Press Co., 1910.

Sweetser, M.F. *King's Handbook of Boston Harbor*. Boston: Houghton, Mifflin & Co., 1888.

Van Wie, David A. *Storied Waters*. Mechanicsburg, PA: Stackpole Books, 2019.

Zwicker, Roxie J. *Haunted Pubs of New England: Raising Spirits of the Past*. Charleston, SC: The History Press, 2007.

ABOUT THE AUTHOR

S am Baltrusis, author of *Ghosts of Salem* and featured in *The Curse of Lizzie Borden* shock doc, has penned more than a dozen paranormal-themed books, including *Haunted Hotels of New England* and *Ghosts of the American Revolution*. He has been featured on several national TV shows, including the Travel Channel's *A Haunting*, *Most Terrifying Places*, *Haunted Towns* and *Haunted USA*. He recently made a cameo in the documentaries *The House in Between 2* and on several television programs, including *Paranormal Nightshift*, *Most Terrifying with Jason Hawes* and *Forbidden History*. He also appeared in *Fright Club* (1 and 2) with the Ghost Brothers and Jack Osbourne on Discovery+. Baltrusis is a sought-after lecturer who speaks at libraries and paranormal-related events across the country. In the past, he has worked for VH1, MTV.com, *Newsweek* and ABC Radio and as a regional stringer for the *New York Times*. Visit SamBaltrusis.com for more information.

Doppelgänger? Author Sam Baltrusis specializes in historical haunts and has been featured on several national television shows sharing his experiences with the paranormal. *Photo by Frank C. Grace.*

FREE eBOOK OFFER

Scan the QR code below, enter your e-mail address and get our original Haunted America compilation eBook delivered straight to your inbox for free.

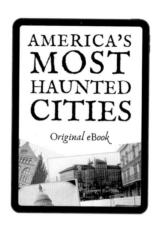

ABOUT THE BOOK

Every city, town, parish, community and school has their own paranormal history. Whether they are spirits caught in the Bardo, ancestors checking on their descendants, restless souls sending a message or simply spectral troublemakers, ghosts have been part of the human tradition from the beginning of time.

In this book, we feature a collection of stories from five of America's most haunted cities: Baltimore, Chicago, Galveston, New Orleans and Washington, D.C.

SCAN TO GET
AMERICA'S MOST HAUNTED CITIES

Having trouble scanning? Go to:
biz.arcadiapublishing.com/americas-most-haunted-cities